The Illustrated Hassle-Free Make Your Own Clothes Book

Joan Wiener Bordow
and
Sharon Rosenberg

Skyhorse Publishing

Skyhorse Publishing books may be purchased in bulk at special discounts for sales promotion, corporate gifts, fund raising, or educational purposes. Special editions can also be created to specifications. For details, contact the Special Sales Department, Skyhorse Publishing, 555 Eighth Avenue, Suite 903, New York, NY 10018 or info@skyhorse publishing.com.

www.skyhorsepublishing.com

10 9 8 7 6 5 4 3 2 1

Library of Congress Cataloging-in-Publication Data

Bordow, Joan Wiener, 1944-
    The illustrated hassle-free make your own clothes book/by Joan Wiener Bordow and Sharon Rosenberg.
        p. cm.
    Previous ed. published: San Francisco : Straight Arrow Books, 1971.
    Order of authors reversed on previous ed.
    ISBN 978-1-60239-309-7 (alk. paper)
    1. Dressmaking. I. Rosenberg, Sharon. II. Title.
    TT515.R8 2008
    646.4'04—dc22
                              2008018860

Printed in China

For Robin
Elana
Daisy
Dandelion
Alissa
Jason
Jerry
Lily
Lola
and Landmark Education

Contents

INTRODUCTION

In 1970, when the original *Illustrated, Hassle-Free Make Your Own Clothes Book* was published, we really did wear the clothes we described in the book—soft velour pants, iridescent, jewel toned velvets, *Little House on the Prairie* dresses. And vests and caps and ponchos, with peyote art colors.

We were sick of the khakis and three-piece suits, Bermuda shorts, Ivy League gear, and drab shirtwaist dresses that turned up in *Life*, *Time*, and *Seventeen Magazine*. Those duds didn't represent us or our dreams and aspirations. We wanted to look like Beau Brummell and pirates and Native Americans. We longed to be fairy princesses, Aragorn and Arwen, Gandalf and Galadriel.

We made our own clothes then because anything we wanted to wear couldn't be bought in a store. The extra perk, of course, was the statement it made.

My first daughter, Shanti Daisy Doe—a sleeping babe-in-arms on the book's original cover—is thirty-eight now, and the mother of my nine-year-old grandchild, Lily Blue. My other girls, Dandelion and Alissa, were yet to be conceived when we wrote the first book. Most of the people who helped create the designs in this book have left San Francisco; many of the couples are divorced, and some of the individuals are gone for good, including our Sharon Rosenberg, whose creative brilliance spawned this book and the others that followed.

My children and their friends remind me of us, nearly forty years ago. They are brilliant, spirited, entrepreneurial, and they question authority. Like then, the times are momentous. Instead of nuclear conflagration, we face environmental devastation. Again, we are embroiled in an insane war in which we are sending our children to fight and die for the interests of rich, old men.

1

We can all use some fun, ease, and play. The ideas and instructions in *The Illustrated, Hassle-Free Make Your Own Clothes Book* may be as relevant today as they were years ago. That's for you to decide.

In any event, I am delighted that this book is being re-issued. I am grateful to my publisher for thinking it worthy of bringing back around.

Have fun and happy sewing!

Love,

Joan Bordow

Sharon Rosenberg wrote this book to share her knowledge of making clothes in a fun and fearless way. Her philosophy was that with a small amount of guidance, you could dress the entire family with style—and for a fraction of the cost compared to store-bought clothing. This book reprint is posthumously dedicated to her daughter, Elana Rosenblatt.

Elana Rosenblatt

Tools

Here are some supplies for the well-stocked sewing kit. The first group are the things you need to begin, the second group those you'll acquire as you go along. When you start a project, buy the things that you need: thread, zipper, snaps or buttons. You're bound to have leftovers and will soon gather a lovely collection of odds and ends for future use.

Things to Start With:

Brown Paper or Paper Bags for making patterns
Needles—assorted sizes
Seam Ripper
Scissors
Straight Pins—large box, medium size
Tailor's Chalk
Tape Measure

Things You'll Acquire:

Beeswax
Buttons
Elastic
Embroidery Needles—assorted sizes
Embroidery Threads
Hooks & Eyes
Leather Needles—assorted sizes
Safety Pins—assorted sizes
Seam Binding
Snaps—assorted sizes
Thread—large spool black
     large spool white
     assorted colors
Zippers

Sewing Machines

If you have a sewing machine—great!—but not having one shouldn't keep you from sewing. In many places, electricity isn't available and it's better not to depend on machines.

Hand sewing is sturdier than machine sewing. It's also a lot more relaxing. What machines can do is shorten sewing time considerably. If you do have access to a machine, don't be afraid to use it. They're extremely simple to operate and can be used for all seam sewing. Hems, however, should always be done by hand.

If you don't know how to use a machine, have someone show you how. This is always better than relying on a diagram.

When using a machine, be careful not to sew in a straight line directly over pins. This can damage the machine. Rather place pins facing the machine's needle, pulling them out before the needle reaches them—or, place pins perpendicular to the needle and sew over them that way.

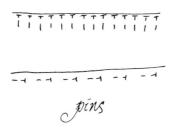

pins

Guide to Illustrations

Dotted line means draw or pin and sew, depending on the context.

Indicates seam on wrong side (inside) of garment, or ragged edges, depending on context.

Indicates gather.

Indicates doubled-over fabric — sides should be aligned exactly (drawings are never exactly aligned in order to show depth).

Indicates hemmed edge.

Terms and Helpful Hints

Casing: This refers to folding over and sewing down the fabric in such a way as to form a tube through which you can string elastic or a ribbon tie—for waistbands on elastic top pants, string gathered necklines or elastic gathered cuffs at wrist or ankle.

Clip Curves: Material sewn on a curve tends to bunch up when worn. Therefore, it's necessary to clip curves at armholes, necklines, crotches, etc. This allows the material to lie flat. Always start your clipping at the ragged edge, cutting up to, but not over, the seam.

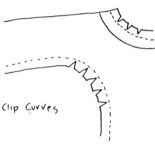

Clip Curves

Darts: We don't use darts on tops because we don't use bras —they give your clothes a funny shape. If you want to make darts, you can figure out easily enough how to add them to the tops. On some pants and skirts, though, darts are useful to make waistbands fit better. You don't have to have them, but here's how in case you want to:

1. On the front, you'll want a small dart about 2″ or 3″ long, going from the waistband out at an angle toward the point of the hip, if you're slim, or straight down toward your belly if that's nice and round.

2. Same in back: make a dart 3″ to 4″ long going from the waist straight down to the part that sticks out the most. This makes things go in where you go in and go out where you go out.

Hold the front piece up to you and mark in tailor's chalk where you want the dart to be. Measure carefully to make sure both darts are an equal distance from the center. Do the same with the back pieces.

3. Fold along the line, right side to right side and sew on a diagonal line, starting at top edge about ½" from fold, down to the bottom of your measured dart. Press flat.

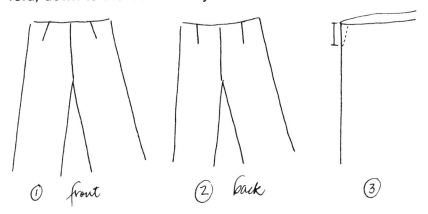

① front   ② back   ③

Elastic: Whenever you use elastic for a waistband or cuff, you can prevent it from curling and twisting if you tack it into place at the sides, front and back of your garment. After the elastic is inserted in the casing, make sure it isn't curled, adjust the gathers evenly, then tack by sewing through the elastic and the front and back of the casing, using a small stitch the way you would sew on a button—it won't show in the folds of the fabric.

Facings: Don't be scared by the word "facing." It is merely an easy way to get a smooth turned edge at garment openings like necks and armholes. The facing is a 2" or 3" piece of fabric that follows the shape of the opening. Instructions

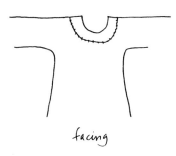

facing

will be given with each pattern where a facing is necessary.

1. Sew the facing into place.

2. Press it out flat, away from the garment. Sew another seam ⅛″ from the first seam, taking in the seam selvage and the facing. Trim selvage. This will help it stay flat and keep it from turning to the outside.

If your fabric is stretchy and pliable, facings aren't absolutely necessary—the ragged edges can be turned under neatly and sewn down. Also, whenever a facing is indicated, you can sometimes use ribbon or lace if you don't have enough extra fabric.

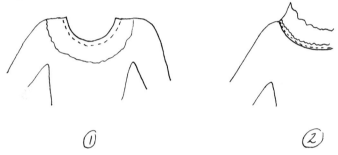

Hem Binding: Ribbon or lace can be used whenever you want to give a smooth, unragged look to hems. It's especially good on heavy fabric where it's hard to turn the ragged edges under.

1. Sew the ribbon to the right side of your fabric so that the ribbon extends just a little beyond the ragged edge.

2. Then turn up your hem to the right length, pin and hem stitch.

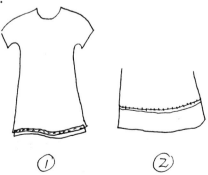

8

Ironing (Pressing): It's good to keep an iron hot and handy while sewing so you can press seams open and flat as you go. You'll frequently find yourself sewing over seams and pressing makes the whole process much simpler.

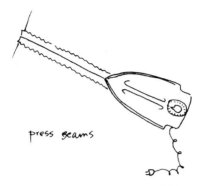

press seams

Reinforcing Seams: Wherever there will be strain on a seam —at the crotch or underarm areas, for example—it is helpful to reinforce this by sewing a piece of ribbon or seam binding over the seam.

    1. Sew the seam as usual.

    2. Pin a piece of ribbon or seam binding over the seam where you want it to be reinforced. Sew over the seam again. Remove the pins and . . .

    3. Clip the curve if necessary, without clipping the ribbon.

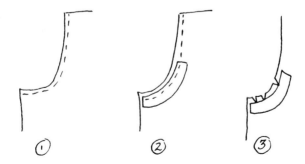

Right Side of Material: This refers to that side of the material which will show when you wear it. It also refers to the opposite of wrong side, not the opposite of left side.

right side

Seam and Hem Allowance: Always remember when cutting out your garment to leave ½-¾" all the way around for seams, facings etc. and 3" or more for hems at the bottom

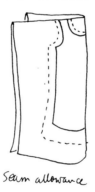

Seam allowance

of pants, tops, dresses, sleeves, etc. If you cut out your garment without a seam and hem allowance, better have a shorter, thinner friend handy to give it to when completed.

Selvage: This is the seam and hem allowance after you sew a seam. It's that little bit extra on the inside of your garment —if it's too wide, it will be bulky so trim it down—if it's too narrow, your seam may start to pull apart. It should be ½-¾" wide on most seams and trimmed down after sewing to ¼-⅛" under facings.

Zippers: If you are using a zipper anywhere besides fly front pants, here is an easy way to do it. If you want a flap covering the coils of the zipper, use the instructions under fly front pants. There are instructions inside the package the zipper comes in for one way of putting in a zipper. Here's another:

1. Sew up your seam, using a basting stitch for where the zipper will lie. Press open.

2. Place your zipper face down on this seam (on the inside of the garment) lining up the coils of the zipper with the seam line. Starting at the bottom, on the inside, sew up one side, checking constantly to see that the coils are still lying true on the seam line.

3. Stitch across the bottom and then up the other side. Using your seam ripper, open up the basting stitches.

You can also put the zipper in by hand. Use the same method of basting the seam. Pin the zipper face down as before. Turn to the outside of the garment and using a tiny back-stitch, sew the zipper into place. Remove the basting and press.

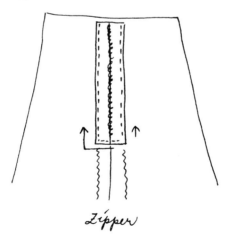

Zipper

Helpful Hints:

Beeswax: This is a really handy, inexpensive thing to have around. It's a circle of beeswax in a small plastic container. When you are sewing by hand, after you thread the needle, pull the thread across the beeswax to coat it—you'll find your thread won't tangle anymore.

Miscellaneous: Buttons, snaps, zippers, etc., are called "notions" in most stores. When you first need to have snaps for something you are making, buy a large card full of assorted sizes; then you have them for the next time. Same with needles and hooks and eyes. Seam Binding is a ribbon which you can use to reinforce a seam, to hem with, or to bind off a seam that will ravel too much. Don't get the kind that irons on—it also falls off. They also sell lace seam binding which is pretty. You can use any kind of ribbon or lace for the same purpose, if you have some at home.

Scissors: You can start with the one you have at home, but a good tool makes your job a lot easier. And the right tool for the job makes it easier yet. First your scissors should be sharp—don't use it for anything but fabric cutting and have it sharpened when needed by a professional. The basic sewing scissors should be about 8-12 inches long—go down to the store, heft a few, and get the largest one that is comfortable for you (that's important). The longer the blade the faster your cutting job will be. Get the best one you can afford —it's worth it.

A pinking shears is a specialty tool. They are expensive and you don't absolutely have to have one. They're also nice to have. Both blades of the scissors are toothed. When you cut the fabric with them, it leaves a toothed edge, one that doesn't ravel very easily, which means less work. Get one only if you really get into sewing a lot—you can do without it.

It's also nice to have a little scissors on hand. These are good for embroidery and for thread snipping while you are sewing. There is a nifty one that has a spring in it—it's only about 4" long and is easy to grab. The spring keeps the little blades apart until you press them together—it's fast and convenient. Again, it's important that the tool be comfortable in your hand and easy for you to use. Buy only one you really think you'll like and use a lot.

Seam Ripper: This is a very handy little tool for mistake correcting and remodeling. If your fabric is delicate, pick through every fourth or fifth stitch the entire length of your seam—the seam should then separate readily and you can start over again. If it's pretty tough fabric, face the ripper down the length of the seam and push—the fast way. You can also use the other end of the ripper to push out the points on sleeves and collars.

Tailor's Chalk: This is a small square of special chalk for fabric—it will brush off easily and won't stain. They come in basic colors, are cheap and handy to have around. They are sometimes sold with fancy little plastic cases to carry them in, but that isn't necessary. A plain tool is a good tool.

Tape Measure: They come in fabric, vinyl and metal. I have found that the vinyl ones last longer and the numbers stay clear—the fabric ones tend to fade and get brittle and worn—the metal ones that roll up into their own container aren't too suitable for fabric and they are more expensive.

Thread: There are many varieties—different weights and materials. If you're really sewing something heavy-duty, get heavy-duty thread. Other than that, medium weight thread is good for most purposes. Silk thread is very strong—it's good for sewing light weight leather and nice for embroidery and top stitching, if you get into that. There are new threads out for stretch fabric and they seem to work—they stretch with the fabric so your seam doesn't pop open and that's nice.

Zippers: There are two basic kinds, nylon and metal, both of which come in light weight and heavy duty. The metal is stronger, of course, but it's also heavier and less flexible. The nylon zippers are really nicer for most clothing, they don't break easily and they're not cold when you lean against them—just don't put a hot iron on them.

Stitches

Back Stitch—This is the most frequently used stitch for making seams. It's best to use a double thread when back stitching. Make a stitch ⅛″ in length. Insert needle into hole at end of first stitch and bring needle through ⅛″ further on. Continue.

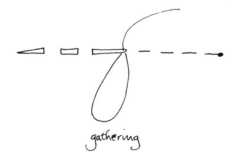

back stitch

Gathering—Take several stitches onto the needle at once, by weaving the point in and out of the material. Push material along thread towards the knot, thereby bunching it up or gathering it to desired length. When gathering a very long

gathering

piece of material, it's a good idea to make two rows of stitches about ⅛″ apart. When material is gathered, hold the ends of your two threads together. That way if one breaks, you won't have to gather all over again. Another way to gather is with pins.

I. Fold the piece you want to gather in half and mark with pins. Keep dividing in halves until you get ⅛ sections marked off. Do the same on the piece you will join the gathered part to.

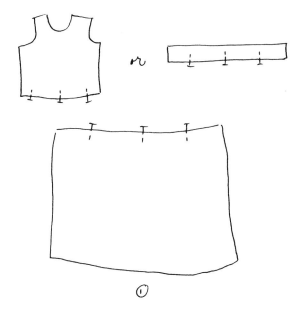

①

2. Pin the two pieces together, right side to right side, matching pins. You will have loops of fabric between each pin that need to be gathered up.

3. Push a little fabric into a gather and pin through both pieces of fabric. Do this again and again until you have the entire garment gathered and pinned, ready for sewing.

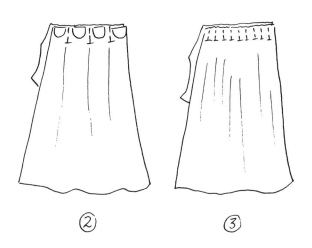

②   ③

Hemming Stitch—A good idea for hemming ragged edges. Make slanted stitches by placing the needle through a tiny bit of material in your garment, then under the hem edge about ¼" away. Your stitches should barely show on the right side of the material.

hemming

Overlap Stitch—This is used when sewing two pieces of leather together, and also in trimming. Make slanted stitches on edge of the material, ¼" apart and ⅛" deep.

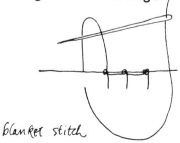

overlap stitch

Embroidery Stitches:

Blanket Stitch—This is used for trimming edges. Make straight stitches on the edge of your material ¼" apart and ⅛" deep, but before pulling thread tight, weave the needle under loop, forming a knot at the edge.

blanket stitch

Chain Stitch—This is used in embroidery. Place needle through fabric. Push needle back into same hole, coming up ⅛" away. Before pulling needle through the material, loop thread around point of needle. Pull needle through the loop, forming the first link in your chain. Repeat, always placing needle back into hole through which you have come. Do not pull chain too tight.

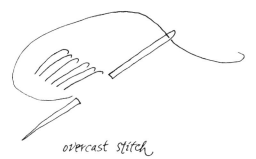

chain stitch

Overcast Stitch—This is used in embroidery, particularly good for filling in large areas. Make stitches one next to the other.

overcast stitch

Trimming Stitches:

Belt Loop—This is used for buttonhole or belt loops. Thread your needle with a quadrupled thread.

    1. Sew a loop on the right side of your material by going back and forth three or four times.

    2. After the final stitch in your loop, take the remaining thread and wind it around the loop as in the

Blanket Stitch (above), leaving the knots on the outside of your loop.

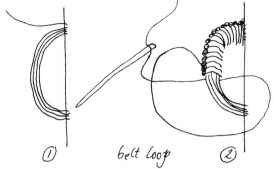

①   belt loop   ②

Tassles—Decide how long you want your tassle to be and cut a number of pieces of yarn twice that length. The more strands you cut, the thicker your tassle will be. Sew strands through your material, right next to one another. Even them out. Tie strands together at the material with another strand of the same length.

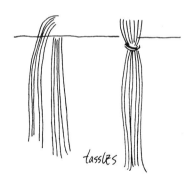

tassles

Embroidery

Sharon was in Formentera without a pair of shoes and the sand so hot on her feet. Under the porch of Mark and Julia's house was an abandoned pair of espadrilles with a hole in the right toe. They fit but she didn't dig the hole. She sewed it up with some wool Julia gave her but thought, "That looks silly." Unbeknownst to her, she had used the Overcast Stitch (see p. 17). So, what she did next was sew a flower onto the shoe. This was her first attempt at embroidery. Then she sewed a butterfly on the left toe to balance out the effect. When the espadrilles wore to nothing, she put the butterfly in a plastic bag which sits in our sewing room in San Francisco.

Embroidery is so easy, you can probably do it with just an idea of what stitches are available and with a few pictures as hints. When something you love is ripped beyond repair, a big butterfly will generally save it. When you dribble spaghetti sauce on your nice white Indian shirt, a big yellow-embroidered sun will make it wearable. Embroidering on your dull old sheets and pillows will help you sleep better. Embroidering on pieces of material in a smart fashion will turn them into wall hangings. There are about 20 million things you can use embroidery for, some of which are illustrated here.

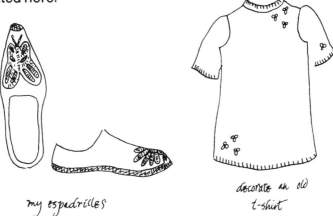

my espadrilles

decorate an old t-shirt

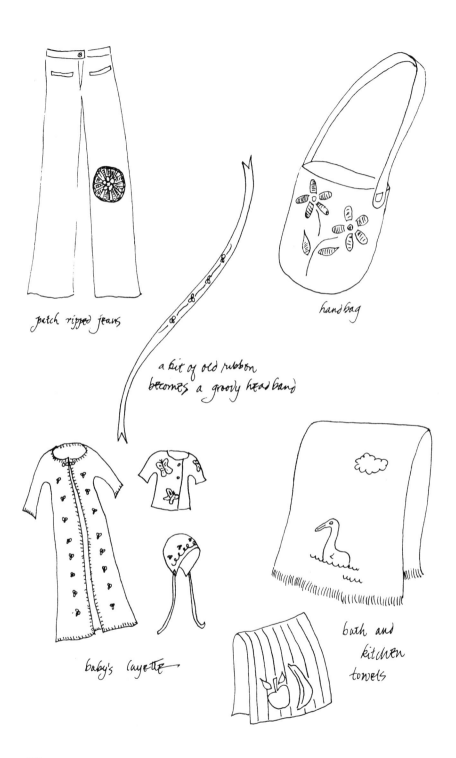

patch ripped jeans

a bit of old ribbon
becomes a groovy headband

handbag

baby's layette

bath and
kitchen
towels

Materials

Certain materials are more conducive to certain garments than others. If you were into wearing a negligee (though we can't imagine why) you wouldn't buy one made out of blue denim.

In any event, after the section on each garment, we've listed what material to use on what garment. Here is the master list in which we've split materials into soft, medium and stiffs. Please refer here if you're hassled over what materials to use.

SOFTS	MEDIUMS	STIFFS
Arnel and related synthetics	Corduroy	Brocade
	Heavy cotton	Denim
Cotton	Heavy velour	Heavy corduroy
Crepe	Satin	Heavy satin
Fine, soft wool	Velvet	Heavy wool
Panne velvet	Voile	Sailcloth
Silk	Wool	Tapestry
Terry cloth		
Velour		

Buying the Right Amount: Most good fabric stores will give you advice about how much to buy, but you should know some basic tips about it so you can judge for yourself.

Fabric is generally made in widths of 36" to 64"— some upholstery and drapery fabrics are even wider. It is sold by the yard and by quarters and eighths of yards— for instance a yard and a quarter, or a yard and five eighths— so you only need buy just what you can use and afford. If the fabric is good and wide, you will probably only need one length in order to make your garment—in other words, for a skirt you may only need the measurement from your waist to the hem plus a little extra for hemming, etc. For slacks, especially wide ones, you may want a length and a half, or even two lengths. You will need about a yard for sleeves and a little extra for facings, hems, and waste. You will gradually learn how to put your pattern on the fabric to use a minimum amount—and how to buy just what you need, which is cheaper. Better to buy generously at first to make sure you have enough.

Grain: As you know, fabric is made up of threads going horizontally and vertically. The threads sort of want to hang straight down. If you put your pattern on the fabric so that the grain and your pattern are going the same direction, your garment will hang on you right—straight up and down. If you angle it off one way or the other, your garment is going to angle off too, and that might not be what you had in mind. Sometimes, however, you will want to take advantage of what fabric will do if you place your pattern on the "bias." This means, instead of putting your pattern straight up and down, you put it on a diagonal. The garment will then drape à la Harlowe. To make something on the bias takes a lot more fabric than to make something on the grain.

Nap: Panne velvet, velvet, corduroy, velour, and terry cloth have what is known as nap. These are little fine "hairs" sticking up to give that nice feel. All these little hairs go in the same direction. If you run your hand down the fabric one way and then back the other way, you can feel a "rough" and "smooth" effect. The way you look at the nap changes the color of the fabric slightly. The important thing to remember in sewing is to get the nap going the same direction all over your garment. If you have the nap going up in back and down in front, you'll look two different colors. If that's what you want, wonderful, but if not, make sure you get them going together.

Taking Care of Materials: First thing to do when you get new material is find out if it's washable. If it is, don't get into the habit of dry cleaning it. Constant dry cleaning knocks the hell out of a fabric and gives it an unpleasant, chemical smell. Clean wash smells and feels a lot better. Also, washing cuts down on non-bio-degradable plastic bags which can end up over the head of your favorite cat or child.

Make sure your fabric can be machine-dried before doing so. Some materials shrink in the dryer. While velour comes out beautifully fluffy when machine-dried, panne velvet shrinks slightly. If you don't know about the drying factor, it's best to wash your material by hand and dry it outside in the sun.

Never wash crepe. Have it dry cleaned. It shrinks and puckers in the wash. It's better to take off crepe clothes before frying potatoes, if you don't like the idea of having them dry cleaned.

Corduroy can be machine washed and dried.

Many brightly colored synthetics should be washed in soap that doesn't contain bleach. Otherwise the colors may wash out.

Most American fabrics have been pre-shrunk, but you should make sure when buying anyway. In Europe, a lot of fabric isn't. Sharon found this out in Ibiza, Spain. She made a full-length muslin dress, then spent many days embroidering irridescent butterflies onto it. After wearing it twice, she washed it out, and it shrank down two sizes. So when buying non-pre-shrunk material, wash it before making it into any clothes.

Recycling Scraps and Waste Materials

At some time or other, everyone has had an indispensable pair of pants—jeans or chinos. And just like Roy Rogers when Trigger died, they are loathe to part with them until the irreversable moment when these pants rip at the knee. Rather than stuffing them—as was Trigger's alleged fate— the pants can be turned into cut-offs by a mere snipping off at the knee. This, then, is recycling in its most common incarnation. Just as organic wastes are recycled, clothing scraps can be used again, old clothes can be magically transformed by a bit of imaginative remodeling, rips can be repaired and all sorts of things can be re-made into perfectly pleasureable, wearable garments without having to be thrown out.

Have a special place where you can save all fabric scraps of substantial size. They're good to use for the following things:

Bags	Pot Holders
Belt Loops	Purses
Bikinis	Ruffles
Bows	Scarves
Collars	Sleeves
Cuffs	Sleeve Extensions
Facings	Stuffed Toys
Hoods	Ties
Kids' Clothes	Ties for Fastening Slits
Panties	Tie Belts on
Patches	Tops and Dresses
Pillows	Trimmings
Pockets	Waistbands
Pouches	and more...

Remodeling Your Old Clothes

1) Neatly cut the sleeves out of tops and dresses, then hem up ragged edges and you have a new, sleeveless garment.

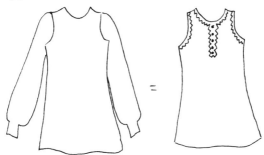

2) For a tank top, cut the sleeves and neck off an old T-shirt and hem up ragged edges. If you want, you can then dye or embroider on it (see p. 16).

3) Take the sleeves off two old shirts and swap them. You'll get two two-tone shirts.
4) Remove and swap collars and pockets from any number of shirts.

5) Re-model the neckline of your old garment—changing it into anything from a scalloped to a boat-neck (see p.71).

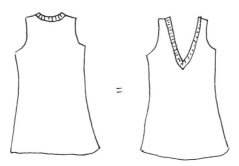

6) Shorten tops, dresses and coats—make shirts into boleros, dresses into tops, coats into jackets.
7) Lengthen tops, dresses and coats by adding a ruffle.

8) Change straight-legged pants into bell-bottoms by slitting the side seams to the knees and inserting a v-shaped piece of material. Let this v be in an interesting pattern or contrasting color.

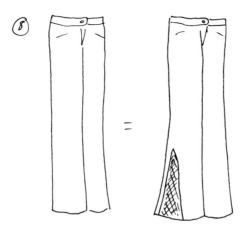

9) When pant-legs shrink from constant washing, sew on ready-made fringe, ribbon, lace or ruffle to lengthen them again. You can even make them longer by adding strips of hemmed, contrasting or matching material.

10) Women can do a whole number by re-modeling a man's sleeveless undershirt. First, try it on. It'll be really large and baggy. Don't fret. Slip a tie or scarf under the arms

in back (this is illustrated). Tie it. The front of the shirt will pull up and the back down into a new thing.

11) Ladies can take another man's sleeveless undershirt, cut the shoulder seams and re-sew the seams to fit. Finish this off by dyeing or tie-dyeing.

12) Embroider on old clothes (see p. 16).
13) Trim old clothes with beads, fringe, lace, etc.
14) Embroider around buttonholes, cuffs and collars (see p. 17).
15) Haunt junk and antique shops for unusual buttons and beads. Remove the old buttons from garments and sew these on.

16) If a top or dress has a back zipper, take the zipper out, hem up the ragged edges and add ribbons or ties as fastenings.

17) Dye or tie-dye old clothes. Get some Rit or Tintex or any common dye. Prepare as directed. Tie garment into knots at various, strategic places. Dip the whole garment into the dye and after it has reached the correct color, remove and rinse as directed. When you untie the knots there will be circles where the knots have been. This is a simple one-color method. There are a few pamphlets and recently published books which will tell you how to really do it up right.

Rips And What To Do About Them

You don't have to throw something out just because it's ripped. Once I threw out an old pair of tights, a *shmata* with a horrifying gash and Sharon said, "Ork. What are you doing?"

"I am throwing this rag away."

"It's still wearable."

Then I take it out and dutifully embroider over the rip and have something I can really dig.

If you don't have a guardian mama-type, heed this: Cover a rip with a super-patch. Richie's jeans ripped in three places. In one place I sewed a patch cut to resemble Saturn, over another rip a crescent moon-patch, over the third a nice leather star.

Embroider something big over a rip—a butterfly, a flower, a crab, anything.

As for ripped tights (panty hose), a ripped seam makes an excellent stem for an embroidered flower. And embroidered tights look groovy even if they aren't ripped to begin with.

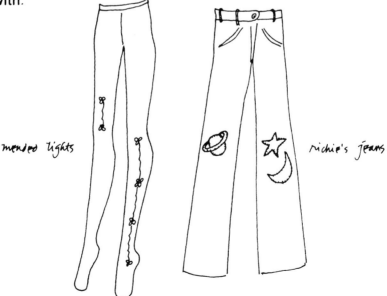

mended tights   richie's jeans

Making Things From Other Things

You can make almost anything from almost anything. Instead of going out and buying new material, try to use stuff that is lying around the house—an unused Indian bedspread hidden in a closet; your old Camp Wip-or-Wil barf green blanket.

Millie and Lou Rosenberg took a cruise to Bermuda and sent their daughter a souvenir of that island—a Greek bag that says "Something Lines" on it. As she already has an Indian mirror bag and another one she borrows from me, she cut off the handles, stuffed it with foam left over from stuffing Ellen's baby's toy and made a pillow.

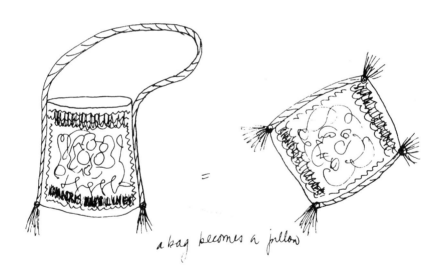

a bag becomes a pillow

For more instances—old terrycloth towels make excellent bath or beach ponchos, or long dresses to stick on after you bathe (see p. 68).

Wip-or-Wil blankets are great for warm ponchos and kaftans (see p. 117).

2 old towels = 1 nice bath/beach dress

Unusable lace tablecloths can be used as dresses, tops, pants.

If you have an old sari, it makes a fine Angel dress (see p.131).

A large scarf can be tied into a warm-weather blouse. Anything, anything, anything. Be bold. If you use something you don't care about in the first place, it doesn't really matter if it doesn't come out perfectly.

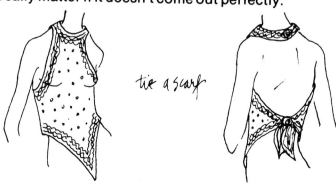

tie a scarf

Patterns

You can use an old well-fitting garment as a pattern, or as a guide to make a brown paper pattern. Using the garment itself as a pattern is super-quick; making a brown paper pattern is a little extra work but you can use it again and again.

The instructions below are for making a brown paper pattern and then using the pattern on your fabric. If you want to use your garment directly as a pattern, the instructions are basically the same, just forget about the paper. Draw the outline of your garment in Tailor's Chalk right on the fabric and cut out, making sure you leave enough for seam allowances and hems.

Before you begin, check your old garment out pretty thoroughly. An examination of the way it was made can give you clues that you may be able to use to make the new one better and longer lasting.

Fold your garment as directed in each of the clothing plans that follow throughout the book. Place it on your paper. Trace the outline of the garment in crayon or magic marker. Remember to always leave ½" extra all around for a seam allowance and an extra 2-3" for hems.

Most important is to measure, measure and measure some more. Measure you (or your friend, if it's for someone else) in different directions, and then measure the pattern you drew to make sure you got it right before you put the scissors to it. It's a nice precaution that sometimes pays off and it's also the way to lengthen, shorten, fatten or slim down the pattern before you start. Cut your pattern out.

Before you pin to your fabric and start to cut out, play with the pattern pieces on the fabric to make sure you can get everything to fit. If your fabric doesn't have a nap, you can put the front going one way and the back going another. If it does have a nap, you have to have everything going the same direction.

When you start to pin your pattern onto your fabric, work on a nice flat surface so you don't get wrinkles and bulges where you don't want them. The floor will do, but a nice table is more comfortable to work at. Pin from the middle of your pattern out to the edges, smoothing everything into place as you go along.

Cut your fabric out carefully around the pattern with a sharp scissors. While you cut, try to leave the fabric and pattern as flat on the table as possible so you don't pull it out of shape.

If you make brown paper patterns, you will soon acquire a "library" of basic patterns: a collection of sleeves, necklines, slacks and dresses that you can mix and match and make into something new.

If you get an idea for something you want to make and really don't have anything around the house to start from, don't be afraid of the patterns you can buy in the stores. A professional pattern can be a good idea for a fancy sleeve or a collar for instance. Certainly it's cheaper and more fun to do it all yourself from something at hand, but the dollar or two that you invest in a basic pattern can be well worth it. You can use the pattern again and again and when it gets too worn, copy it in brown paper for your collection.

Clothes for Women—Skirts

Ten-minute Long Skirt

1. Measure from your waist to the desired length—mini, midi, maxi. Double this amount and add an extra 6″. This is the amount of material you'll need.

Fold material in half widthwise, right side to right side. Cut material on fold. You will have two squares.

2. Align squares right side to right side with pattern or nap running in same direction. Pin together down sides ½″ from edge. Sew over pins. Remove pins. Press seams.

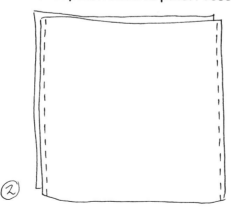

3. Fold over top and pin. Turn edge under about ¼"
and pin. Remove first set of pins. Make sure there is enough
room for your elastic to go through. Sew edge around, leaving
1" open at front to put through elastic.

Take elastic and measure your waist. Don't pull it
tight, rather make sure it is comfortable. Allow 2" extra for
overlap. Cut elastic.

Pin one end of elastic to skirt near opening. Attach a
safety pin to other end of elastic and snake elastic through
edge of skirt. Remove pins. Overlap the ends and sew
securely. Sew skirt top closed. Or, you might want the
elastic to be adjustable or use a drawstring instead. In that
case, leave about 6-8" extra on elastic and tie, leaving the
unsewn 1" on waist open. Remove pins.

Turn up bottom edge of skirt and hem. You might
want to finish off the skirt hem by sewing on lace edging or
seam binding.

Twenty-minute Variation

Make a Ruffle-Bottom Skirt by following Steps 10-13, Ruffle-Bottom Dress. The ruffle looks special if made of contrasting material.

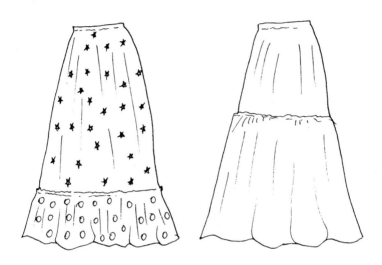

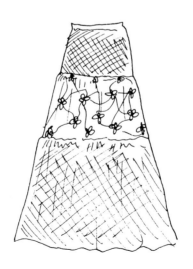

A-Line Skirts

The A-line skirt is almost as basic as the gathered skirt. It is simple but you will need to make darts.

1. Take a comfortable skirt that fits you well. Fold in half and place along the lengthwise fold of your material. Using Tailor's Chalk, draw around the skirt, allowing enough room for seams and hems.

2. Fold in half for the back and place on the fabric, draw around as before. Cut out your pattern pieces.

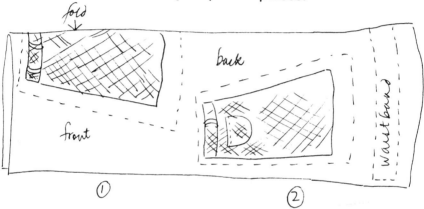

3. Take the front piece (the one that was on the fold) and hold it up to you. Mark with tailor's chalk where you would like the darts to be. Check these marks with your tape measure to make sure they are an equal distance from the center of the garment. Sew darts and press. Do the same with each back piece.

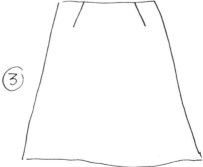

4. Place the 2 back pieces together right side to right side. Sew the back seam. Use a loose basting stitch for the 7 or 9" at the top of the seam, (this is where your zipper will go), and a firm stitch for the remainder of the seam. Press the seam open.

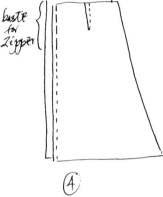

5. Lay your zipper flat down on your seam, making sure the outside of the zipper is facing the outside of the garment. Pin in place, with the coils of the zipper lying directly on top of the seam line. Sew in place by hand or machine. Use your seam ripper to remove the basting stitches.

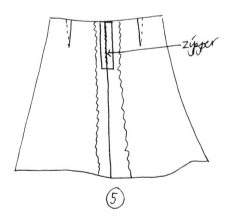

6. Place the front and back together, right side to right side, and pin. Try on and adjust. Sew side seams.

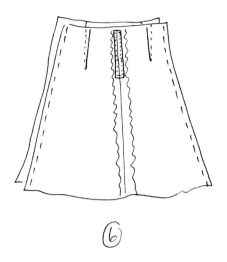

6

7. Measure your waist for waistband. Cut a piece of fabric the length of your waist measurement plus two or three inches for a tab, and two and ½ inches wide. Starting at one side of zipper opening; pin to your garment, right side to right side. Sew. Remove pins.

7

8. Turn waistband down over inside seam, tuck ragged edge under, pin and hem down. Turn ragged edges in at closing edges of waistband and hem. Attach hooks and eyes. Try on and pin for hem. Hem.

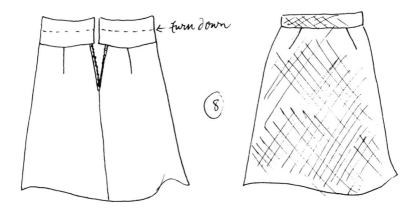

If you would rather not have a waistband, or want a skirt that hip hugs, use a ribbon facing instead. Just sew the ribbon all around the top of the right side of skirt. Then sew another seam all around the top edge, through the facing and the selvage to hold it down flat. Turn facing inside, press flat. Tack at seams or hemstitch.

If you don't have an A-line skirt to work from, it is fairly easy to draw a pattern from scratch.

1. Measure your waist. Divide by 4 and add one inch for darts. Draw this length horizontally against the edge of your brown paper.

2. Measure how long you want the skirt, adding 2 or 3 inches for a hem (more is good, you can always cut it down).

Mark this point on the edge of the paper.

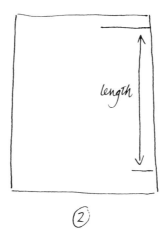

②

3. Estimate how wide you want the edge of the skirt to be—one way is to stand as if you were mid-step and then measure around where the bottom of the skirt will be. Add a few inches to be sure, and mark this length horizontally at the bottom point of the skirt.

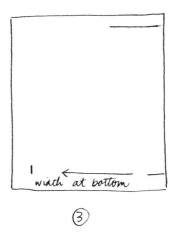

③

4. Draw a diagonal line from the waist to the hem.

42

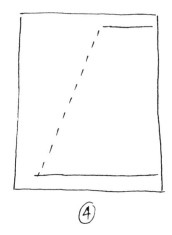

④

5. Check your hip measurement and compare with the same place on the pattern to make sure you have allowed enough room. Adjust. Cut out.

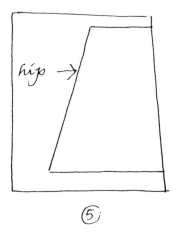

hip →

⑤

This one pattern piece will do for both front and back: cut the front out on a lengthwise fold of the fabric and the back away from the fold.

Clothes for Women—Pants

Basic Elastic-Top Pants

Take a pair of comfortable old pants. In many cases, this will be a pair of well-worn jeans. If the top you want on your new pants differs from the tops of the old ones (ex. you are copying an old pair of waist pants and want hip-huggers), pin down your old pants to the top desired or add the necessary number of inches to the top when drawing the shape of pants on your material. The crotch measurement is pretty important if you want the pants to fit well. To make sure you get it right, sit down on your tape measure in a nice flat chair. Pull the tape measure up to your waist in front and to your waist in back. Then measure the front and back crotch on the pattern to make sure it's not too long or too short. If it's too short, it won't feel good, and will wrinkle, if it's too long, it'll look really baggy.

1. Get a piece of material 2 ½ yds. long (3 yds. long if you are really tall). Fold material in half lengthwise, right side to right side. Pin edges.

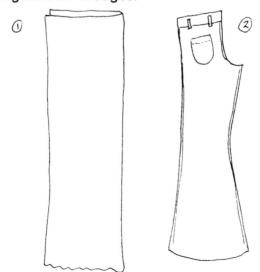

2. To draw back of pants—fold your old pants front to front. Make sure side seams are properly aligned. Pin neatly. Make sure the crotch is sticking out.

3. Lay old pants on material. Pin. In chalk, trace old pants onto material. Make allowances for seams and hems, plus about 2″ extra to width at the hips or waist area (so that pants will slip on and off easily). Remove pins and pants from material.

To draw front of pants—fold your old pants back to back. Follow Steps 2 and 3. (Make sure to place front and back onto material in the same direction, so that nap, texture, or pattern of fabric goes the same way.) Cut out new pants.

4. Take one front piece and one back piece. Pin them together right side to right side at leg seams, leaving crotch curve open. Repeat this process with remaining front and

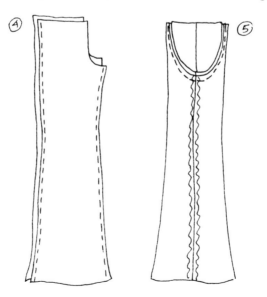

back piece. Now try on the legs and make sure that they fit. If not, re-pin. Sew leg seams together ½" from edge.

5. Place one pants leg into the other, right side to right side, aligning seams, and sew the crotch seam. Reinforce the crotch seam with ribbon or seam binding if you wish. Turn both legs inside-out.

Try the pants on and see how high you want the top.

6. Fold over top and pin. Cut edge even, if it is ragged. Turn the ragged edge under about ¼" and pin. Remove first set of pins. Make sure there is enough room for your elastic to go through. Sew edge around, leaving 1" open at front through which to put elastic.

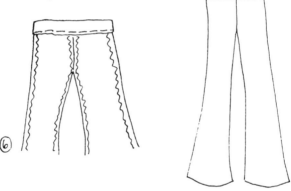

Take elastic and measure your waist or hips (wherever you want pants). Don't pull it tight but make sure it is comfortable. Allow 2" extra for overlap. Cut elastic.

Pin one end of elastic to pants near opening. Attach a safety pin to other end of elastic and snake elastic through edge of pants. Take off safety pins, overlap ends of elastic and sew securely. Tack. Sew pants top closed. You might want the elastic to be adjustable or use a drawstring instead. In that case, leave about 6-8" extra on elastic and tie, leaving the unsewn 1" on waist open.

Turn up bottom edge of legs and hem. You might want to finish off the legs by sewing on edging lace or seam binding.

Turn pants right-side out.

Basic Elastic Top Pants Without Side Seams

Once you make this pattern you can turn out slacks for yourself and friends in about two hours, start to finish—and they fit and look good! It's a one-piece pattern, so there is a minimum of pinning, cutting and sewing. You will need a double length of fabric.

1. Draw a center line down the length of your brown paper.

2. Take your hip measurement at the widest part and draw it across the top, horizontally with the center line. This is your waist line (which will be gathered—it has to be your hip measurement so you can get them on). Draw a second line two and ½ inches above this for your elastic casing.

3. Take a favorite pair of slacks. Fold them at the front crotch. Do the same for the back crotch on the other side.

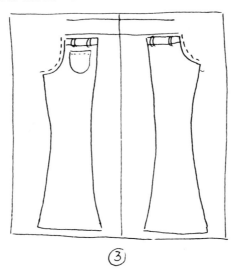

③

4. Now measure from your waist to your ankle, plus hem allowance. Draw a horizontal line at the bottom of your pattern that is this distance from the waist line.

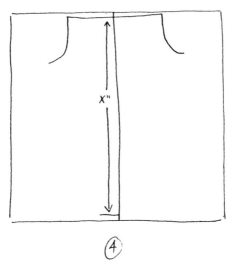

X"

④

5. Draw straight down from the bottom point of the crotch to the hemline. If you want the pants to flair more,

draw this as a diagonal line out to how wide you want the pants at the bottom. Now you have a paper pattern.

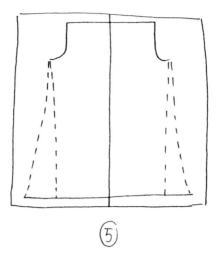

(5)

6. Fold your fabric widthwise, right side to right side, place your pattern on it in line with the grain, pin and cut with a sharp scissors. If your fabric has a definite nap, or a pattern running in one direction, fold material in half width-wise and cut on fold. Realign the fabric with nap or pattern going in the same direction.

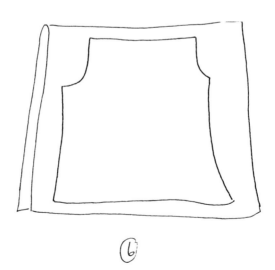

(6)

7. When you finish cutting, your front and back crotch seams will be lined up ready for sewing. Sew your front crotch seam, then your back crotch seam. Reinforce with ribbon if you wish.

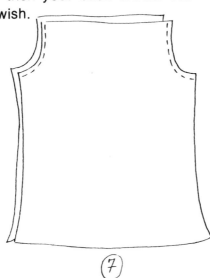

8. Open garment and realign by bringing front and back crotch seams together. Pin leg seams, right side to right side and sew.

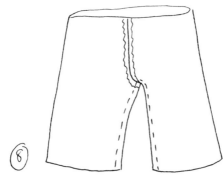

9. Turn top edge down towards inside and tuck in ragged edge to form elastic casing. Pin and sew, leaving an opening to insert your elastic through.

Measure the elastic against your waist. Allow 2" for overlap and cut. Pin one end of elastic to pants near opening.

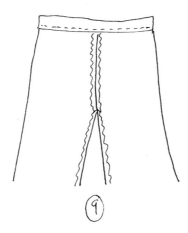

Attach safety pin to other end of elastic and snake elastic through the casing. Remove pins. Overlap the ends of the elastic and sew together securely. Sew opening closed. Try on for length and hem.

To use your basic pattern for other friends, just work from your center line to make it wider or thinner. Check the crotch measurement and the length, and cut accordingly.

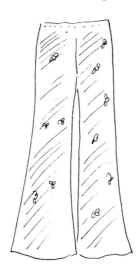

Fly-Front Pants

Take a pair of your comfortable old pants, as in Basic Elastic-Tops.

1. Follow Steps 1 through 3 as in Basic Elastic-Tops. Then when drawing front of pants, draw in a fly-piece as illustrated.

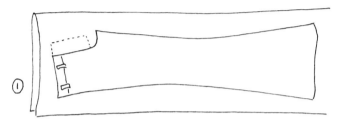

2. As with Basic Elastic-Tops.

3. Place one pants leg into the other, right side to right side, aligning seams. Sew the crotch seam up to the fly-piece. Turn both legs right-side out.

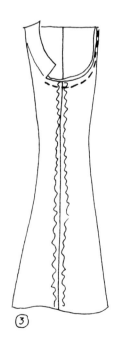

4. Fold left fly-piece about ½″ back from the front seam.

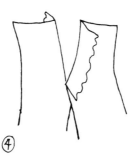

5. Get a zipper to fit opening (about 7″ for waist pants, 5″ for hip-huggers). Open it. Place left side of zipper on left fly-piece so that zipper sticks out over fold about ⅛″. Pin zipper to fly-piece. Sew along edge. Remove pins. Close zipper.

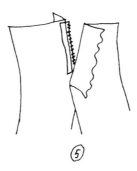

6. Fold right fly-piece back so it is aligned with crotch seam. Pin to zipper about ¾″ from that fold.

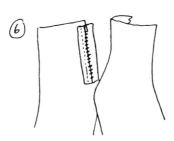

7. Sew over pins. When you sew to the bottom of the zipper, stitch diagonally across until you reach the crotch seam.

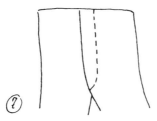

Iron seams flat. Turn ragged edges under and sew them down. Turn pants right-side out.

You can have a button front fly, if you want. Make the fly the same way, but put button holes on the outside and sew buttons in place on the inside part of the fly. To make buttonholes, use the blanket stitch *very* close together in a buttonhole shape, slit open.

Waistband

With a tapemeasure, measure all the way around top of pants. Add 2" to this amount. This is the length of your waistband. Decide how wide you want waistband. Multiply this width by two plus 1", for waistband width. Cut this shape on a piece of unfolded material. Sew two pieces of material together, if necessary, to get this shape.

If your pants are hip-huggers, a good way to make the waistband fit you exactly without sticking out in the back is:

1. Fold waistband widthwise, right side to right side. Or, cut it into two equal pieces. Sew a seam line as illustrated.

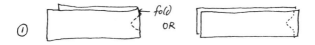

2. Align top of waistband with top edge of pants. Starting from right side of fly, leave about 1½" of waistband

over pants edge and pin waistband to pants, right side to right side, placing pins ½" from top all the way around. Sew over pins. Remove pins.

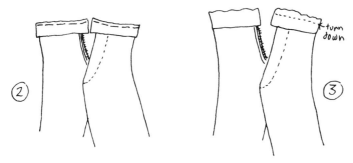

3. Turn waistband up and press. Now, turn waistband half-way down and press. Turn pants inside-out. Turn ragged edges of waistband under and hem. Turn ragged edges in at closing edge of waistband and hem. Turn pants right side up. Sew snaps or hooks and eyes to closing edge of waistband.

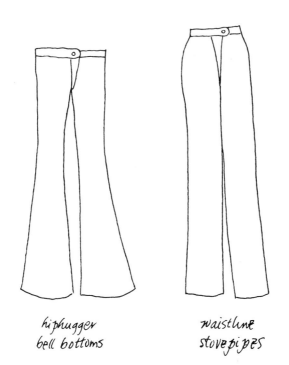

hiphugger
bell bottoms

waistline
stovepipes

Belt Loops

Decide how wide and long your belt loops will be and how many loops you want. Loops can be made out of the same pants material or something complimentary. Here's how to determine how much material to set aside for loops. If you want 6 loops, 2" long by 1" wide, multiply 6 by 2 plus an extra 3" for hemming. In this case, your piece of material should be 15" long by 1" wide.

1. Fold material in half lengthwise, right side to right side. Pin sides together ⅛" from edge. Sew over pins.

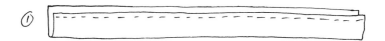

2. You now have a tube. With a chopstick or pencil, push this tube through itself so it comes right-side up. Press tube. Cut as many pieces as you want, as long as you want it. Each of these pieces will become a loop.

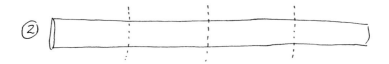

3. Turn ragged edges of each loop under and sew to waistband.

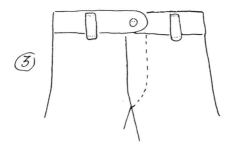

Cuffs

Decide how wide your cuffs will be. Add 2" to this width. When drawing your pants onto material, add this amount to the bottom of each leg. After you hem the edges of pants bottoms, turn up cuff. Press very well. Tack cuff at side seams (see Tacking under Terms).

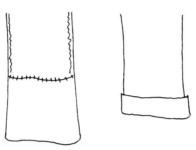

Patch Pockets

Decide how large your pockets will be.

1. Cut a square that size, adding an extra ½" all the way around.

2. Which edge do you want to use as the top for your pocket? Turn it under twice and hem.

3. Turn other edges under and sew to your garment.

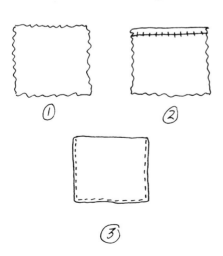

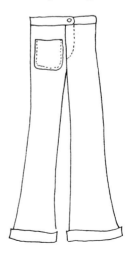

Bellbottom Pants

If you are tracing your new pants from an old pair of bellbottoms, follow Steps for either Elastic-Tops or Fly-Fronts exactly. If, however, your old pants aren't bells, follow Elastic-Top steps 1 and 2.

3. Lay old pants on material. Pin. Trace your old pants in chalk onto material down to knees. Then taper your line out diagonally, anything from a regular modified bell to super-wide bells, down to the bottom of pants leg.

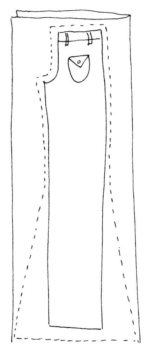

Continue as for Elastic-Tops or Fly-Fronts.

Ruffle Pants (That Look Like a Skirt)

Follow Steps 1 and 2 for Elastic-Tops.

3a. Lay the old pants on material. Pin. In chalk, trace old

pants onto material down to knee. Remove. Fold old pants back to back. Pin and trace to knee. Measure width of new pants at knee. Multiply this width by four. Decide how long you want new pants, plus seam and hem allowance. Cut out two identical pieces of material which are above-width by above-length.

3b. Fold each piece in half widthwise, right side to right side. Pin ½″ from edge. Sew over pins. Remove pins. You now have two tubes.

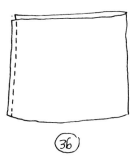

Follow Steps 4 through 6 for Elastic-Tops. Do not turn up legs to hem.

7. Turn pants right-side out. Gather tube at one end (see Stitches) to match width of knee.

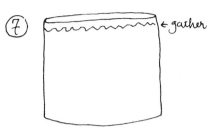

8. Place gathered edge of tube over knee of pants, right side to right side. Pin. Sew over pins. Remove pins. Flip tube over. Turn up bottom edge of legs and hem.

Sexy Slit Pants With Bows

Follow Steps 1-3 for Elastic-Tops or Fly-Fronts.
4a. Take 1 front piece and 1 back piece. Pin them together from waist to thigh. Pin inside leg seam. Repeat this process with remaining front and back piece. Try on the legs, making sure they fit. If not, re-pin. Sew legs together over

pins. 4b. Turn ragged edge under on leg slits and hem.

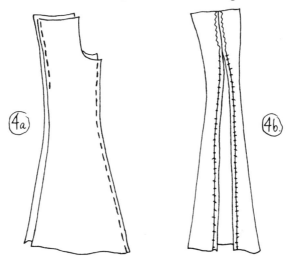

Follow Steps 5 and 6.

7.   Decide how large you want your ties to be and how many you want. You'll need two strips of material for each tie. Mark along wrong side of slit wherever you want ties to be. Sew one tie to either side of slit, over marks.

Tie side bows when wearing.

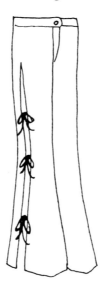

Materials for Pants:
(See Materials, p. 21)

Basic Elastic-Tops: Softs.
Fly-Fronts: Mediums and Stiffs.
Bellbottoms: Softs, Mediums, Stiffs.
Ruffle Pants: Softs.
Sexy Slit Pants: Softs, Mediums, Stiffs.

Clothes for Women—Tops And Dresses

We've put tops and dresses in one section because they are interchangeable. Depending on how you wear your clothes, a longish top can be worn as a very mini-dress or a dress can be worn with pants as a top.

Basic Top or Dress With Large Round Neck

1. When acquiring your material, decide how long you want the garment, double this amount and add an extra 6" for hem. Then decide how long you want your sleeves. If you want long sleeves that are part of the top rather than added on, get very wide material. Since extra bread for wide material can be a problem, another solution is to add an extra piece of material for the sleeves while tracing new garments. Sometimes this looks much groovier. You can even contrast materials. In any event, fold material in half widthwise, right side to right side.

2. Fold material in half lengthwise. Pin along open edges.
3. Take a top or dress that fits you comfortably. Fold it in half down the front. Lay old garment on material so top is

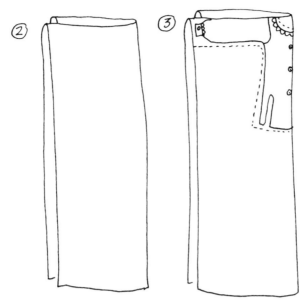

aligned with top fold of material, center is aligned with center fold. Pin garment to material.

4. Trace old garment onto material allowing for seams and hems starting from edge of sleeve and going straight

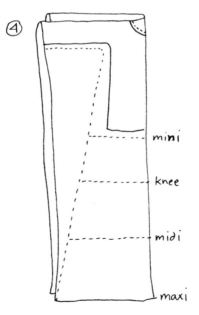

mini

knee

midi

maxi

across to the armpit. At armpit, draw a wide curve going from under the arm, diagonally down to the bottom of the garment, as long as you wish.

When drawing the neck, follow the neck size of your old garment drawing a small curve.

Remove old garment from material, leaving material pinned. Cut out new garment.

Neck Facing:

5. From scraps, cut a 1" square of material. If no such size scrap is available, piece two scraps together. Fold in quarters.

6. Lay facing over the neck matching the edges. Pin facing to garment. Draw a curve in facing to match the neck curve. Then remove pins and facing from garment. Cut neck curve on facing.

7. Cut the squared edge of facing from corner to corner, following the contour of the curved end of facing, as illustrated.

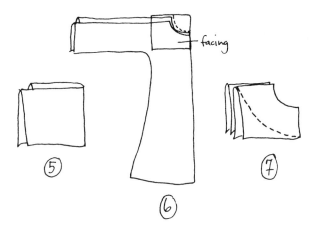

8. Open up the piece of clothing. Open up your facing. Place facing to garment, right side to right side, matching holes. Pin facing to garment. Place pins ¼" from hole. Sew facing to garment over pins. Remove pins. Clip curves (see

Terms). Cut any excess material from seam.

Facing is now on the outside of the garment. Fold it inside. Trim edge if necessary. Turn ragged edges under and hem.

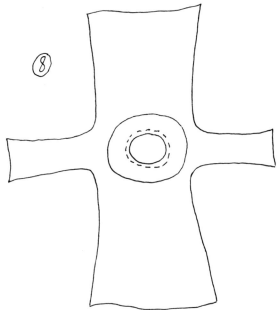

9. Fold garment at neck so that it's inside-out, aligning front and back. Starting at the edge of one sleeve, pin a ½" seam all around, leaving bottom open. Repeat at other sleeve. Sew over, then remove pins. Clip curves. Press seams. Turn up bottom and hem. Turn up sleeves and hem. Turn garment right-side out.

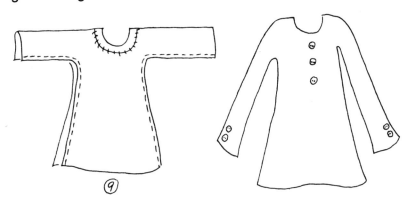

Sorceror's Top or Dress

1. Decide how long you want the garment, double this amount and add an extra 6" for hem. You'll need wide material since the sleeves are one part of the same material as the top. Fold material in half widthwise, right side to right side.

Follow Steps 2-3 for Basic Top.

4. Follow size of old garment in chalk but draw in a long sleeve by starting your chalk 2' down open edge of material and drawing a diagonal up to the armpit curve. Follow curve around armpit and draw down to the hem, tapering out diagonally, as illustrated.

Follow through Step 9 for Basic Top.

Flower Top or Dress

1. As in previous directions, decide how long you want the garment, double this amount and add an extra 6" for hem. You'll need wide material as sleeves are one with top. Fold material in half widthwise, right side to right side.

Follow Steps 2-3 for Basic Top.

4. Follow size of old garment but draw in a long sleeve by starting l' down open edge of material and drawing a diagonal up to the armpit curve. Follow curve around armpit and draw down to the hem, tapering out diagonally, as illustrated.

Follow through Step 9 for Basic Top.

You can attach ribbons or tassles to the bottom point of sleeves.

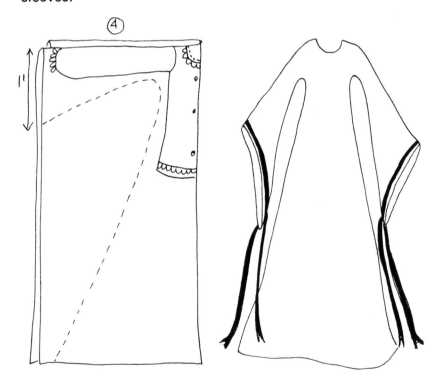

Hobbitop

Follow Steps 1-9 Flower Top.

When hemming bottom of sleeves, leave enough room to put through elastic. Hem sleeves, leaving ½" open to put elastic through.

Measure one wrist with elastic, allowing 1" for overlap. Cut elastic. Repeat with other wrist. Attach a safety pin to one end of elastic and snake through sleeve hem. Overlap ends of elastic and sew securely. Repeat with other sleeve and sew the openings closed.

Ruffle-Bottom Dress

Decide what type of dress you want—Basic, Sorceror's, Flower. Decide how long you want dress to end before adding ruffle—mini, midi, maxi.

Follow steps 1-9 but don't hem bottom of dress.

10. Measure width of dress at bottom. Multiply this

width by four. Decide how long you want ruffle to be. Cut a piece of material to this measurement.

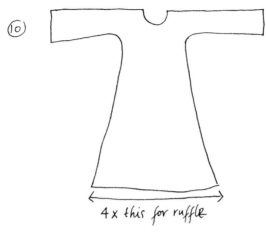

4 x this for ruffle

11. Fold material in half widthwise, right side to right side. Pin ½" from edge. Sew over pins. Remove pins. You now have a tube. Gather tube at top end (see Stitches) to match width of dress bottom.

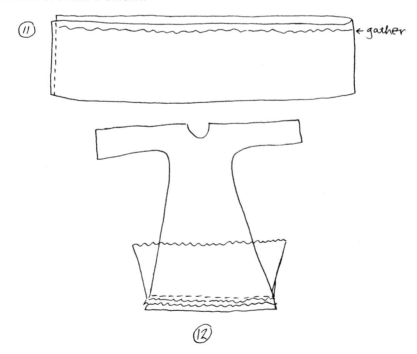

← gather

12. Place garment right-side out. Place tube inside-out. Place tube over bottom. Pin and sew over. Remove pins.

13. Flip tube over. Turn up bottom edge of ruffle and hem.

Speedboat Neck Top or Dress

Follow Steps 1-3 Basic Top.

4. Trace an old garment onto material, allowing for seams and hems, starting from edge of sleeve and going

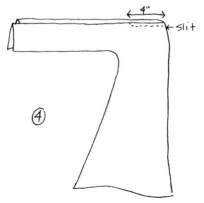

straight across to the armpit. At armpit, draw a wide curve going from under the arm, diagonally down to the bottom of the garment, as long as you wish.

For the neck, make a slit along the top fold of material, from center to a point 4" away.

Remove old garment from material, leaving material pinned. Cut out new garment.

5. Open up your garment. Turn ragged neck edge under and hem.

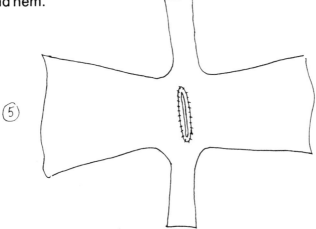

6. Fold garment at neck so that garment is inside-out, aligning front and back. Starting at the edge of one sleeve, pin a ½" seam all around, leaving bottom open. Repeat at other sleeve. Sew over pins. Remove pins. Clip curves (see Terms). Press seams. Turn up bottom and hem.

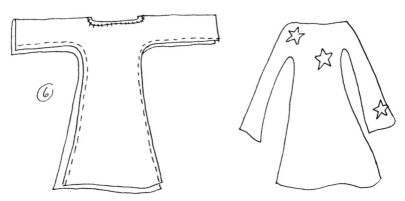

Scalloped Neck Top or Dress

Follow Steps 1-7 Basic Top.

8. Open your garment. Open the facing. Draw scalloped curves onto facing, as illustrated.

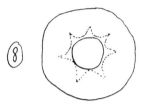

9. Pin facing to garment right side to right side, matching holes. Place pins ¼" from hole. Sew over pins, following scalloped curves. Cut away excess material. Clip curves. (see Terms.)

Facing is now on the outside of garment. Fold it inside. The scalloped curves will have to be pushed through with a little help from a chopstick or pencil. Press scallops. Trim edge if necessary. Turn ragged edges under and hem.

Follow Step 9 Basic Top.

If your top has a scalloped neck, you might want to add scalloped cuffs also.

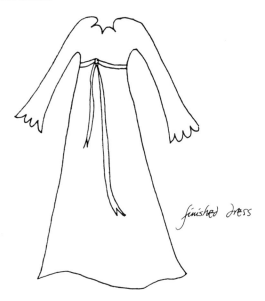

finished dress

Scalloped Cuffs

1. Cut two pieces of material 3″ wide by the length of your sleeve edge.

2. Pin right side of material to right side of sleeve.

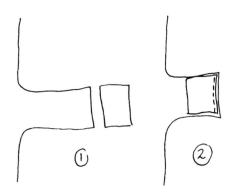

3. With chalk, draw a scalloped edge on each piece of material. Sew following scalloped curves. Cut away excess material. Clip curves.

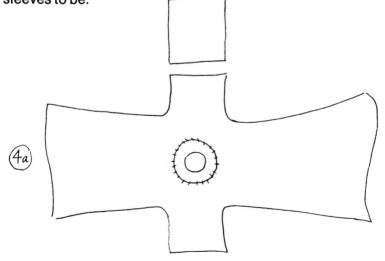

Scalloped cuffs are on the outside of garment. Turn them under, pushing scalloped curves through with chopstick or pencil. Press scallops. Trim edges if necessary. Turn ragged edges under and hem.

Add-On Sleeves

Long Add-Ons

4a. At Step 4 Basic Top, cut two pieces of material as wide as sleeves on your garment by as long as you wish sleeves to be.

4b. Sew sleeve pieces to sleeves, right side to right side.

4c. Press seams flat. Sew seam edges down. This makes the sleeve look like a false French seam.

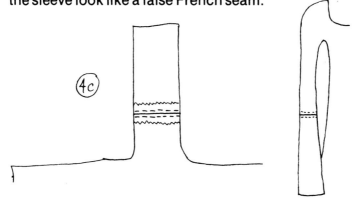

Continue with rest of Step 4-9.

Ruffled Add-Ons

4a. At Step 4 Basic Top, cut two pieces of material twice width of each sleeve on garment by as long as you wish sleeves to be.

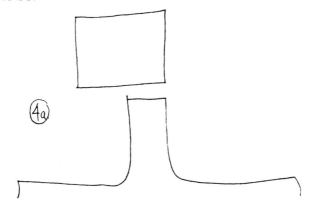

4b. Gather one end of each piece of material to match width of garment's sleeves.

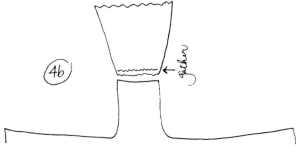

4c. Pin right side of sleeve piece to right of sleeve on each side of garment. Sew over and remove pins. Press seams.

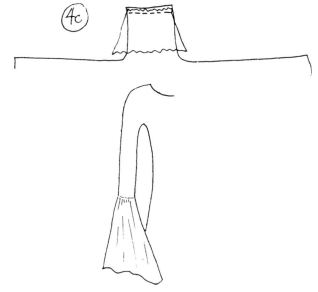

Double-Gathered Add-Ons

Follow Steps 4a-4c, Ruffled Add-Ons.

At Step 9 Basic Top, before hemming bottom of sleeves, leave enough room to put through elastic. Hem sleeves, leaving ½" open to put elastic through.

Measure one wrist with elastic, allowing 1" for overlap. Cut elastic. Repeat with other wrist. Attach a safety pin to one end of elastic and snake through sleeve hem. Overlap ends of elastic and sew securely. Repeat with other sleeve. Sew openings closed.

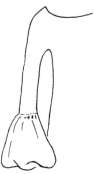

Top or Dress With Small Round Neck

Follow Step 1-3 Basic Top.

4. Trace old garment onto material, allowing for seams and hems, starting from edge of sleeve and going straight across to the armpit. At armpit, draw a wide curve going

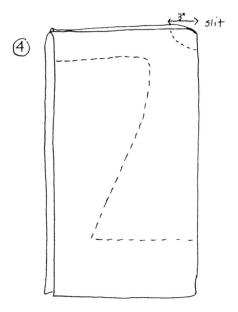

from under the arm, diagonally down to the bottom of the garment, as long as you wish.

For the neck, make a slit along the top fold of material, from center to a point 3″ away. Mark a curve following the neck contour of your old garment, as illustrated.

5. Remove old garment from material, leaving material pinned. Cut out the rest of your garment but not neck curve. Open up your garment. Fold it lengthwise down center. Now, cut along chalked neckline to slit. Mark center fold where cut edges are, as illustrated.

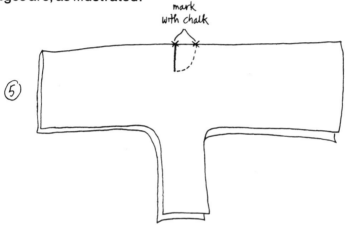

Neck Facing:
6. From scraps, cut a rectangle of material 1′ x 18″. Fold in half lengthwise.

To allow your head into this garment, there has to be a slit at the neck, either in the front or back. Decide where you want it.

7. For a front slit, place facing on folded edge of garment so that 3″ extend above slit in garment and the large portion of facing is below the curve. Pin facing to garment. Cut

facing to match garment's neck opening. Remove pins. Remove facing.

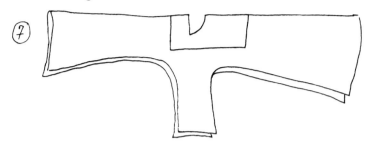

8. Cut facing as illustrated.

front slit

9. For a back slit, place facing on folded edge of garment so that 3″ extend below the garment's curve with the large portion of facing above the slit. Pin facing to garment. Cut facing to match garment's neck. Remove pins.

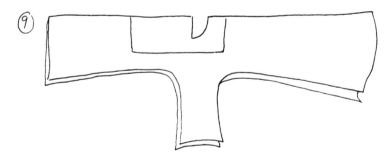

10. Remove and cut facing as illustrated.

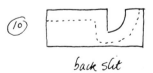

back slit

11. Open up your garment. Place right side of facing to right side of garment, matching holes. For a front slit, long rectangle of facing will be below the garment's curve. For a back slit, long rectangle will be above straight edge of garment's neck opening.

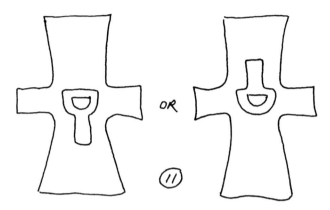

OR

12. Pin facing to garment ¼" from hole. Do not pin completely around hole, but rather as illustrated. Sew over and remove pins.

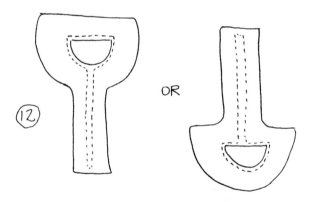

OR

13. Cut a straight line from bottom of curve to ¼" from the seam on rectangle. Clip curves at bottom of slit and neck, as illustrated (see Terms).

Your facing is now on the outside of your garment.

Fold it inside. Trim edge if necessary. Turn ragged edges under and hem.

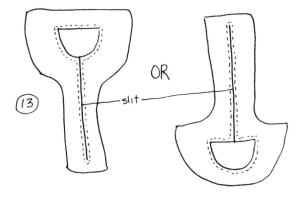

14. Fold garment at neck so that garment is inside-out, aligning front and back. Starting at the edge of one sleeve, pin a ½" seam all around, leaving bottom open. Repeat at other sleeve. Sew over pins. Remove pins. Clip curves. Press seams. Turn up bottom and hem. Turn up sleeves and hem. Turn garment right-side out.

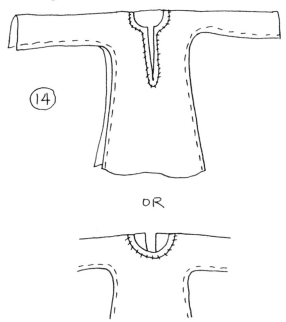

Sew a fastening to the top of slit. This can be two pieces of material to form a bow (either front or back slit), or a hook and eye or button and loop (see Stitches) if in back.

finished dress

Wurdleturdleneck Top or Dress

Follow Steps 1-5 Small Round Neck.

6. From available scraps, cut a rectangle of material 2″ x 5″. Place facing on straight edge of garment's neck right side to right side, extending up. Pin facing to garment.

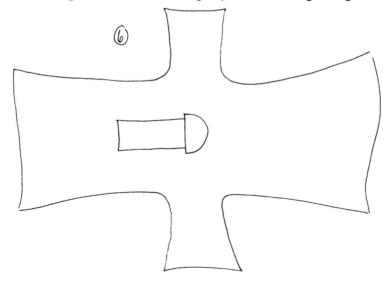

7. Draw a straight line down center of rectangle. Starting from the neck edge of garment, sew facing to garment, as illustrated.

Cut down chalk line to a point 2" from bottom of facing, cutting through facing and garment. Clip curves at bottom of slit, as illustrated.

Your facing is now on the outside of your garment. Fold it inside. Trim edge if necessary. Turn ragged edges under and hem.

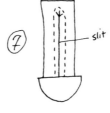

8. With a tapemeasure, measure all the way around top of neck edge. Add 2" for overlap. This is the length of your turtleneck collar. Decide how wide you want the collar. Double this width and add 1". Cut this shape out on unfolded material.

Starting from one edge of the top of neck slit, leave 1" over slit edge and pin collar to neck opening, right side to right side, placing pins ¼" from top. Pin all the way around.

Sew over pins. Remove pins. Turn collar up and press.

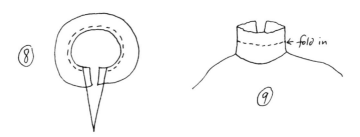

9. Fold collar at half way point towards inside of garment.

10. Turn ragged edges of collar and hem on inside neck-

line. Sew snaps or hooks and eyes to closing edge of turtleneck. Skip to and follow Step 14, Small Round Neck.

Forties Fold Back Collar Top or Dress

Follow Steps 1-5 Small Round Neck.

6. From scraps, cut a rectangle of material 1' x 18". Use a contrasting material if you want an interesting effect. Fold in half lengthwise.

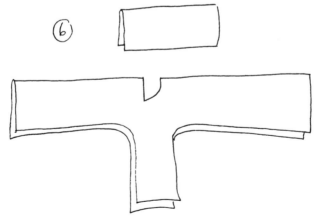

7. Place facing on folded edge of garment so that 3" extend above slit in garment, large portion of facing is below

curve. Pin facing to garment. Cut facing to match garment's neck opening. Remove pins. Remove facing.

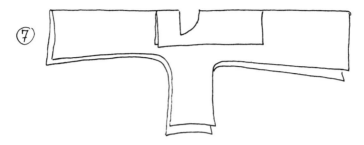

8. Cut facing as illustrated.

Following Steps 11-14 Small Round Neck.

15. Fold back sides of neckline at slit to form lapel collar. Tack corners (see Terms).

Sleeveless Top or Dress

This top can either be left sleeveless or with an added set-in sleeve.

1. Get 2 yds. of material for Sleeveless Top, plus another 1 yd. for set-in sleeves. Because of the armholes in this top, the front and back will be sized slightly differently. So, lay material down right-side up. Fold one side of material over, as illustrated for front of dress.

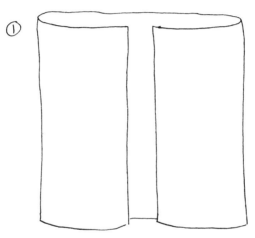

2. If possible, use a sleeveless garment for tracing. If you don't have anything sleeveless, pin old garment sleeves under at armpit and tuck sleeve out of the way when tracing.

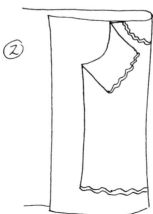

To draw front of garment, fold old garment with top fold of material, center fold with center fold. Pin garment to material.

3. Trace old garment onto material, allowing for seams and hems, starting from the shoulder. When you get to under the armpit, taper line out diagonally, as long as you wish as illustrated.

For Neck, follow neckline of old garment, drawing a small curve. If you want a lower neckline, draw a bigger curve.

Remove garment but leave material pinned. Fold over other side of material for drawing back of dress. Fold old garment in half down the back. Lay on material, aligning top with top fold, center with center fold. Pin garment to material.

Trace old garment onto material as front, allowing for seams and hems. Remove garment from material, leaving material pinned.

4. Cut out front and back of top. Pin front and back together at shoulders, right side to right side. Sew over pins. Remove pins.

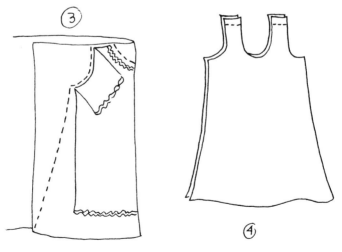

5. Open top and fold lengthwise, as illustrated, matching shoulder seams and neck opening.

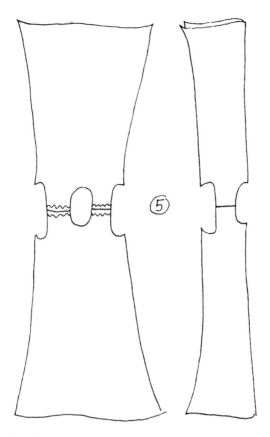

Neck Facing:

6. From scraps, cut a 1' square of material. Fold in half.

7. Place facing over neck hole in top. Pin. Cut a curve in facing to match curve in neck of garment. Remove pins. Remove facing.

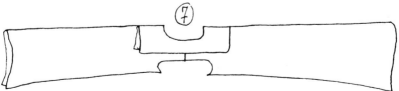

8. Cut the squared edge of facing from corner to corner, following contour of the curved end of facing, as illustrated.

9. Open up your garment. Open up your facing. Place facing to garment, right side to right side, matching holes and pin. Place pins ¼" from hole. Sew over and remove pins. Clip curves (see Terms). Cut any excess material from seam.

Facing is now on outside of garment. Fold it inside. Trim edge if necessary. Turn ragged edges under and hem.

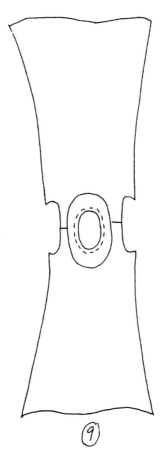

10. Fold garment at neck so that dress is inside-out, aligning front and back.

Starting under the armpit, place pins down sides of top. Fit top on, adjusting pins if necessary. Sew over pins. Remove pins. Press seams. Turn ragged edges under at arms. Hem armholes and bottom of garment. If you wish to have an armhole facing you can make one exactly the same way you make a neck facing, but it is not necessary.

finished dress

Josephine's Variation

Tie a ribbon under the bust, tacking it down in back (see Terms) or holding it in place with sewn-on loops.

Josephine's Variation

Set-in Sleeves

Set-in sleeves tend to be a bit difficult, as far as selecting correct sleeve-size goes. So buy the cheapest pattern you can get for a dress with a plain, set-in sleeve. Trace this sleeve pattern onto sturdy brown paper and keep it with your sewing paraphernalia.

Follow Steps 1-10 Sleeveless Top. Do not hem armholes.

11. Get a yard of material. Fold in half widthwise, right side to right side. Place pattern on material. Pin pattern to material. Cut out sleeves. Remove pins. Remove pattern.

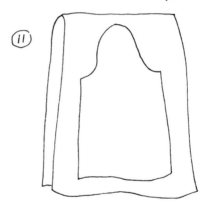

12. Fold each sleeve in half lengthwise, right side to right side. Pin arm seams. Sew over and remove the pins. Press seams flat.

13. Turn sleeves right side out.

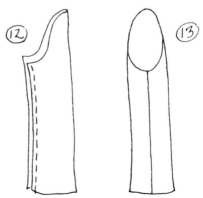

14. Turn garment inside-out. Place sleeves inside garment, aligning at underarm seams. Pin sleeves around armhole ½" from edge. Sew over pins. Remove pins.

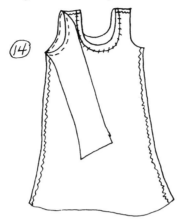

15. To secure sleeve in garment, sew another curve, close to edge where sleeve and dress are joined, as illustrated. Clip close to this second seam. Pull sleeves inside-out. Turn ragged edges of sleeves under at cuff and hem.

Set-in Variation I

Follow Steps 1-10 Sleeveless Top. Do not hem armhole.

11. For a short or ¾ length sleeve, cut out sleeves as illustrated. Follow Steps 12-15 as Set-in Sleeve.

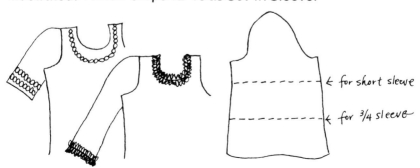

for short sleeve

for ¾ sleeve

Set-in Variation II

Follow Steps 1-10 Sleeveless Top. Do not hem armholes.
11. For a wide sleeve, cut out sleeves as illustrated.
Follow Steps 12-15 as Set-in Sleeve.

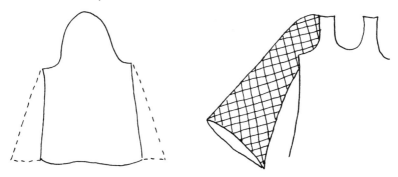

Set-in Gathered Sleeve

Follow Steps 1-15 Set-in Variation II. Before hemming sleeves, leave enough room to put elastic through. Hem sleeves, leaving ½" open on hem to put elastic through.

Measure one wrist with elastic, allowing 1" for overlap. Cut elastic. Repeat with other wrist. Attach a safety pin to one end of elastic and snake through sleeve hem. Overlap ends of elastic and sew securely. Repeat with other sleeve. Sew openings closed.

Set-in Short, Puffy Sleeve

Follow Steps 1-10 Sleeveless Top. Do not hem armholes.
11. Cut a short, puffy sleeve as illustrated.

Follow Steps 12-15 Set-in Sleeve. Before hemming sleeves, leave enough room to put through elastic. Hem sleeves, leaving ½" open to put elastic through.

Measure arms with elastic, allowing 1" for overlap. Cut elastic. Do safety pin number as above. Sew opening closed.

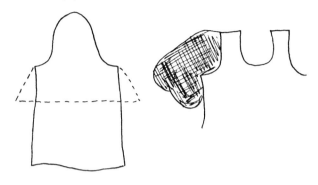

Set-in, Gathered-at-Shoulder Sleeve

Follow Steps 1-10 Sleeveless Top. Do not hem armholes.

11. Get a yard of material. Fold in half widthwise, right side to right side. Place pattern on material. Pin pattern to material. Chalk onto material an extra 2" curve at the top of each sleeve, as illustrated. Cut out sleeves. Remove pins. Remove pattern.

12. Fold each sleeve in half lengthwise, right side to right side. Pin arm seams. Sew over pins. Remove pins. Press seams flat.

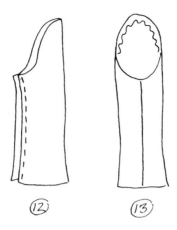

13. Gather each sleeve at top so hole of sleeve matches armhole of garment. Turn sleeves right-side out.

Follow Steps 14-15 Set-in Sleeve.

Waistcoat

Waistcoats can be made in any length from bolero-style to maxi.

1. Get 1 yd. of material, unless you desire a very long waistcoat. In that case, get 2 yds. or 2½ yds. depending on your height (measure from your shoulders to the floor for specific yardage). Lay material down lengthwise right-side

up. Fold one side of material over, as illustrated, for front of waistcoat.

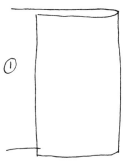

2. If possible, use a sleeveless garment for tracing. If you don't have anything sleeveless, pin old garment's sleeves under at armpit and tuck sleeve out of the way when tracing.

To draw front of garment, fold old garment in half down the front. Lay on material, aligning top of garment with top fold of material, center fold with center fold. Pin garment to material.

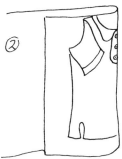

3. In chalk, trace old garment onto material, allowing for seams and hems, starting from the shoulder. When you get to under the armpit, draw straight down to the hips. If you want your waistcoat to go beyond the hips, taper line out diagonally when you get to under the armpit, as long as you wish, as illustrated.

For neck, follow neckline of old garment, drawing a small curve.

Remove garment but leave material pinned.

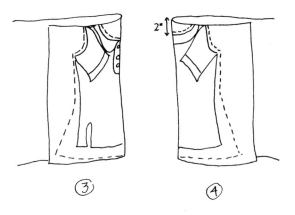

③ ④

4. Fold over other side of material for drawing back of waistcoat. Fold old garment in half down the back. Lay on material aligning top with top fold, side with center fold. Pin garment to material.

Trace old garment onto material as front. For the neckline, starting 2" down from top of center fold, draw a small curve upward, as illustrated.

Remove garment but leave material pinned.

Cut out front and back.

5. You have cut two pieces, as illustrated. Fold front piece in half and slit on fold.

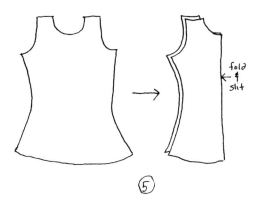

fold
slit

⑤

6. Pin two front pieces to back piece at shoulders and sides, right side to right side. Try garment on, adjusting pins if necessary. Sew over pins. Remove pins. Press seams flat.

Turn ragged edges under at armholes, around neck and down front opening. Hem.

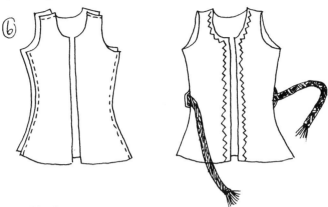

Waistcoat Variations

Your waistcoat can be made in a variety of shapes and lengths. Some of them are illustrated. Before hemming ragged edges under at neckline, play around with the neck shape and cut to suit your imagination.

Factory Worker's Jacket

1. Get 2 yds. of material. If you want a very long jacket, measure from your shoulders to wherever you think the jacket should reach, then add a yard for sleeves. Lay material lengthwise, right-side up. Fold one side of material over, as illustrated, for front of jacket.

If possible, use a sleeveless garment for tracing. If you don't have anything sleeveless, pin the old garment's sleeves under at armpit and tuck sleeve out of the way when tracing.

To draw front of garment, fold old garment in half down the front. Lay on material, aligning top of garment with top fold of material, center fold with center fold. Pin garment to material.

2. Trace old garment onto material, allowing for seams and hems, starting from the shoulder. When you get under the armpit, draw straight down to hips. If you want the jacket to go beyond your hips, taper line out diagonally when you get under the armpit, as long as you wish, as illustrated.

For neck, follow neckline of old garment, drawing a small curve.

Remove garment but leave material pinned.

Cut out front.

Fold over other side of material for drawing back of jacket. Fold old garment in half down the back. Lay on material, aligning top with top fold, center with center fold. Pin garment to material. Trace old garment onto material as front. For the neckline, draw a small curve upward (illustrated in Waistcoat Step 4) starting 2″ down from top of center fold.

Remove garment but leave material pinned.

Cut out back.

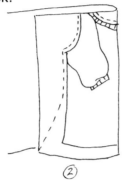

3. You have cut two pieces, as illustrated.

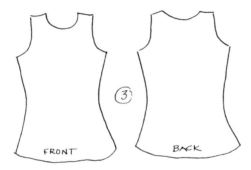

FRONT   BACK

4. Fold front piece in half and slit on fold.

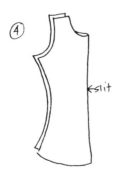

←slit

5. Pin two front pieces to back piece at shoulders, right side to right side. Sew over pins. Remove pins. Press seams flat.

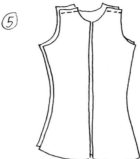

6. Open up new garment and lay it flat.

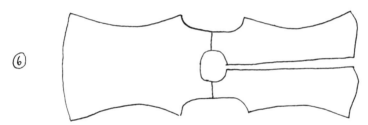

7. Fold it in half lengthwise, aligning neck opening and front opening, right side to right side.

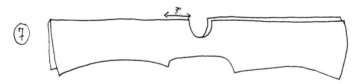

Neck Facing:

8. Measure garment from bottom of front edge to 3″ past the neck opening. Cut a rectangle of scrap material this length by 1′.

9. Fold facing in half. Align bottom edge of facing to bottom edge of jacket. Pin facing to garment. Cut facing to

match jacket's neck opening, as illustrated. Remove pins. Remove facing.

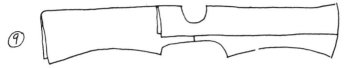

10. Cut facing as illustrated. Slit down fold under neck opening. Do not slit fold above neck opening.

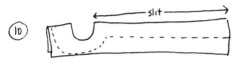

11. Open up your jacket. Place right side of facing to right side of jacket, matching holes. Pin facing to jacket ¼" from neck opening. Sew over pins. Remove pins. Clip curves.

Your facing is now on the outside of your jacket. Fold it inside. Trim edge if necessary. Turn ragged edges under and hem.

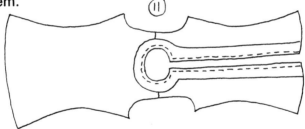

12. Fold jacket at shoulders so it is inside-out, aligning front and back. Pin sides ½" from edge. Try jacket on, adjusting pins if necessary. Sew over pins. Remove pins. Press seams flat.

13. Turn jacket right side out. Fold back sides of neckline at opening. This will form a lapel collar. Tack corners (see Terms).

⑬

Sleeves:

Follow Steps 11-15 Set-in, Gathered-at-Shoulder Sleeve. Vary length of sleeves, cutting them short, mid-length or long.

Materials for Tops & Dresses:
(See Materials, p. 21)

Basic Top: Softs, mediums, stiffs.

Sorceror's Top: Softs. Preferably anything floppy—purple velour and black panne velvet are super.

Flower Top: Softs. Arnel prints are groovy.

Ruffle-Bottom Dress: Softs, mediums, stiffs. Ruffle might be in a contrasting fabric or color to dress, and should be floppy and soft.

Speedboatneck Top: Softs, mediums.

Scalloped Neck Top: Stiffs so that scallops will stand up.

Small Round Neck Top: Softs, mediums, stiffs.

Wurdleturdle-neck Top: Softs, mediums, stiffs.

Forties Fold Back Collar: Softs, mediums, stiffs.

Sleeveless Top: Softs, mediums, stiffs.

Josephine's Variation: Softs, mediums or stiffs will do but soft floppies are best.

Waistcoat: Softs, mediums, stiffs. Use imagination. Sharon made a super waistcoat of reversable green velvet.

Factory Worker's Jacket: Softs, mediums, stiffs. Best are velvets, brocades and tapestries.

Ten-Minute Long Skirt: Softs, mediums. If your material is too stiff, it will bunch up at the waist. Look for some bright, floral prints.

Clothes for Women—Teeny-Weeny Bikini

Bikini Top:

1. To insure the proper breast shape, it's best to make a pattern first out of some old material scraps.
   Cut an equilateral triangle 6" x 6" x 6". If your breasts are bigger, make a larger triangle.

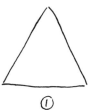

2. From bottom center of triangle, chalk a line that goes to the center. Cut out along this line.
   Fit triangle over one breast, pinning sides of slit to make triangle fit. Fit this triangle over other breast. If it doesn't fit (or if individual breast sizes are slightly different), cut out a second triangle and re-fit.
   Make chalk lines over pins at slit. Remove pins.
   Line up triangular pattern so that slit comes together as it did before cutting.
   Get ½ yd. of the actual bikini material.
   Fold material in half, right side to right side.
   Place triangle pattern or patterns on material. Pin. Cut two triangles for each breast. Transfer chalk lines on pattern to bikini material. Remove pattern. Cut center slit on each triangle.

3. Fold all four triangles in half separately, right side to right side, aligning chalk lines. Place pins on chalk lines. Sew over pins. Remove pins. Press darts.

4. Take the two right-breast triangles. Place them together, right side to right side. Pin two sides of the triangle, ¼" from edge. Leave 1" open at bottom of each side through which to put tie. Sew over pins. Remove pins.

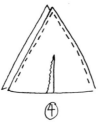

5. Turn triangles right side out. Fold ragged edges on bottom inside.

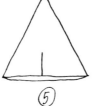

6. Place pins along bottom ⅛" from edge. Sew over pins. Remove pins.

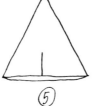

7. Place pins ½" from this line. Sew over pins. Remove pins.

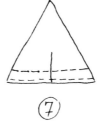

Repeat Steps 4-7 for two left-breast triangles.

Using either contrasting ribbon or ties made from your bikini material, measure ribbon or ties all the way under bust from front to back. Allow several inches excess for tying bow. Cut this out.

Snake ribbon or tie through bottom of each triangle.

Attach a piece of ribbon or ties to top edge of each triangle, long enough to go around neck and tie.

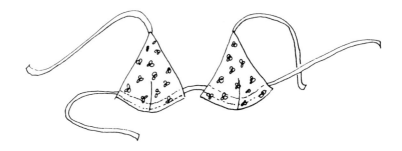

Bikini Bottom:

1. To cut bottoms, sacrifice an old pair of underpants and use them for a pattern. If they are not bikinis, cut them down to desired fitting.

Open side seam of underpants and remove elastic.

Get ½ yd. of material.

Fold material in half right side to right side. If you don't want the bottoms to be lined, don't fold material in half and don't follow instructions for sewing two bottom pieces together.

Lay underpants flat on material, as illustrated. Pin underpants to material.

Trace underpants onto material, allowing ¾" for seams and hem. Remove underpants from material. Cut material along chalk lines.

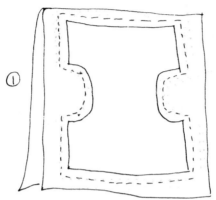

2. Fold each piece in half, right to right, aligning sides. Place pins along sides ½" from edge. Sew over pins. Remove pins.

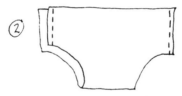

3. Place one bottom piece inside other, wrong side to wrong side, and work with pieces as if they were really one piece. Turn ragged edges ⅛". Turn again ½". Pin around top and leg at edges. Sew over pins, leaving ½" open at top and at each leg opening to put through elastic.

Measure the elastic around your hips and the top of each leg. Allow 1″ extra for overlap at each measurement. Cut elastic.

Attach safety pin to one end of each piece of elastic. Snake elastic through openings. Overlap ends and sew securely. Sew openings closed.

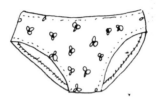

Materials for Bikinis:

Quick-drying fabrics—synthetics, terrycloth—but above all, make sure they are washable.

Clothes for Women—
Dorothy Lamour's Road to Bali Sarong

This is something you can wear as is or over your bikini. If made to wear over a bikini, use the same material.

Measure from your waist to ankles.

Take a piece of material this long that wraps comfortably around your body.

Turn all edges under and hem.

Wrap material around your waist and tie top two corners together at either side or at center over bust, as illustrated.

Clothes for Men

The relationship between men's and women's clothes is extremely close and constantly overlapping. We swap shirts, sweaters, trousers, bush jackets, belts with our old men without even thinking about "Oh, this is a chick's scarf," or "Wow, I can't wear this, this is my old man's shirt. It buttons the other way."

There was once a time which everybody's buttons were on the same side. Then came swords. It was decided to change the buttons on men's coats and jackets to the right side so that they could easily unbutton their clothes with the left hand. This freed the right hand and made the drawing of the sword (which was *always* worn on the left) a much quicker process. Well, we don't know many cats walking around with swords on nowadays, so we can't see any reason for going thru changes about which side to put the buttons on men's clothing. Even shops are carrying men's pants with elastic-tops—once considered a totally feminine thing.

For these reasons, we decided not to put in separate descriptions and plans for the making of men's clothes. Instead, we refer you to chose styles in the Clothes for Women section which are the most appropriate to consult.

Pants—Basic Elastic Top Pants (extra good for doing Yoga in or gardening).
Fly-Fronts
Bellbottoms
Shirts—To make a men's shirt, refer to the section on Tops. There's one minor difference between making tops for men and women—for men, instead of tracing the old garment from under the arm diagonally down to the bottom of the garment, trace it *straight* down to the bottom of the garment . . . or take a man's tapered shirt for tracing and use that shape.

elastic top pants   fly front pants   with cuffs, pocket & belt loops

basic top

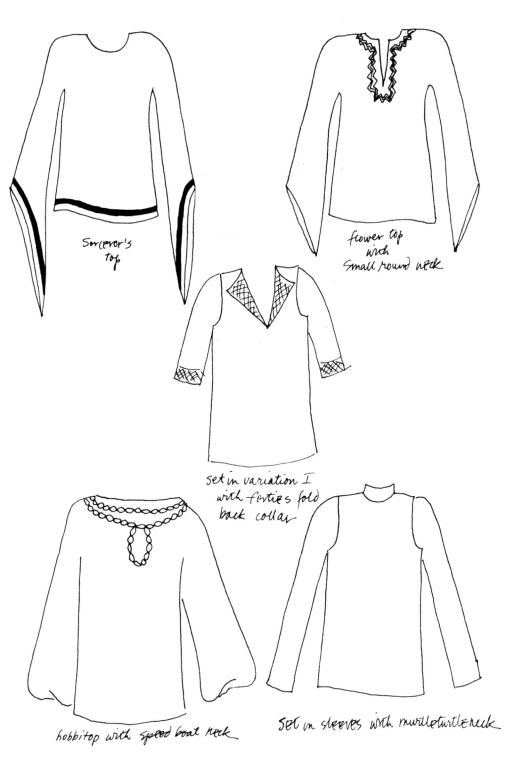

Sorceror's top

flower top with small round neck

set in variation I with forties fold back collar

hobbitop with speed boat neck

set in sleeves with muffleturtleneck

114

Set in variation II
with speed boat neck

Set in gathered sleeves with
small round neck

set in gathered at shoulder sleeves
with large round neck

TEENY WEENY BIKINI BOTTOMS

115

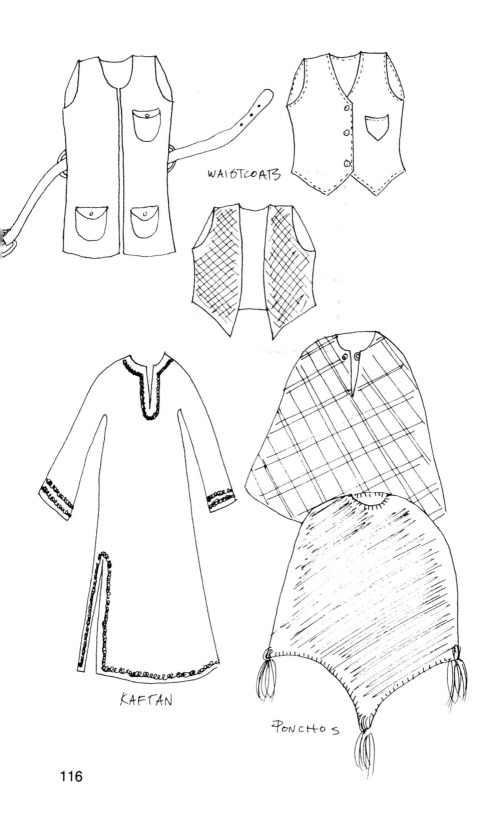

WAISTCOATS

KAFTAN

PONCHOS

116

AC-DC Clothes

Kaftans

1. Decide how long a kaftan you want, double this amount and add an extra 6″ for hem. Then, figure how long you want the sleeves to be. If you want them to be part of the kaftan, rather than added on, get very wide material. If not, you can easily attach Add-On sleeves.

Fold material in half widthwise, right side to right side. Fold in half lengthwise. Pin along open edges.

Take a top that fits you comfortably. Fold in half down the front. Lay old garment on material so top is aligned with top fold of material, center is aligned with center fold. Pin garment to material.

Trace the old garment on the new material, chalk kaftan about 3″ larger than old garment as kaftans are meant to be worn over clothes.

When drawing neck, follow the neck size of your old garment, drawing a small curve.

Remove old garment from material, leaving material pinned.

Cut out kaftan.

Neck Facing:

2. From scraps, cut a 1' square of material. If no such size is available, piece two scraps together. Fold in quarters.

Lay facing over neck on kaftan, matching the edges. Pin facing to kaftan. Cut a curve in facing to match neck curve of kaftan. Remove pins. Remove facing from kaftan.

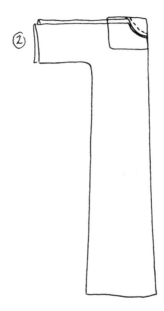

3. Cut the squared edge of facing from corner to corner, following contour of the curved end of facing, as illustrated.

4. Open kaftan. Open facing. Place facing to garment, right side to right side, matching holes. Pin facing to kaftan ¼" from hole.

Sew facing to garment over pins. Remove pins. Clip curves. Cut any excess material from seam.

Your facing is now on the outside of your kaftan. Fold

it inside. Trim edge if necessary. Turn ragged edges under and hem.

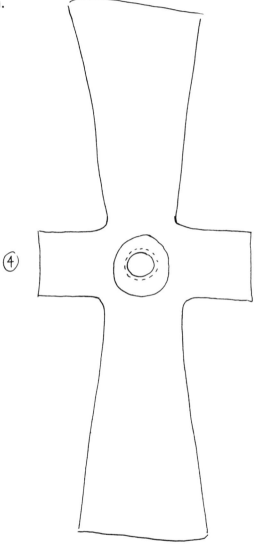

5. Fold kaftan at neck so that it is inside-out, aligning front and back. Starting at the edge of one sleeve, pin a ½" seam all around until you get 1' from bottom at each side (or more if you want a longer slit). Repeat at other sleeve.

Sew over pins. Remove pins. Clip curves. Press seams. Turn ragged edges under at slits and bottom and hem.

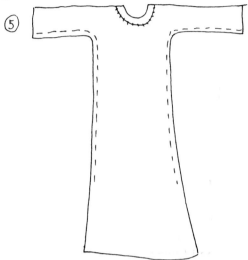

Kaftan Necklines:

You may use any type of neck for your kaftan. If you want it to have a hood, as well, follow the instructions for Top with Small Round Neck (with slit in front). When tracing kaftan, remember to draw it 3″ larger than old garment. Also remember to leave a slit on either side of kaftan's bottom.

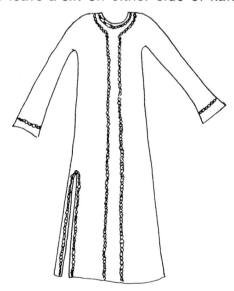

Kaftan Hood I:

1. Cut two squares of material 18" x 18". Pin squares together, right side to right side.

2. Draw a small curve on edge of your material, about 9" in, as illustrated. Cut material at curve.

Place pins, as illustrated, ½" from edge of hood. Sew over pins. Remove pins. Press seam, turn ragged edges at seam under and hem. Turn and hem rest of ragged edges.

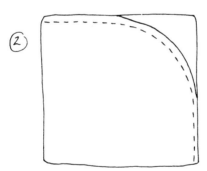

3. Align hood with kaftan, right side to right side, starting at one side of the kaftan's neck opening slit.

Pin hood to kaftan 1/3 of the way around on each side. Leave back unpinned.

The unpinned section of the hood will be larger than the remaining neck space on kaftan. Gather hood section to match neck opening. Pin hood to kaftan. Sew over pins. Remove pins. Sew down all ragged edges on inside of hood.

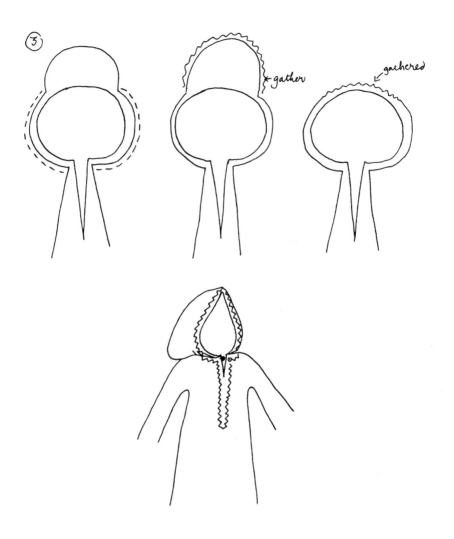

Kaftan Hood II:

1. Cut two squares of material 2' x 2'. Pin squares together, right side to right side.

Measure the kaftan's neck opening by starting from one end of the slit opening and measuring around to other side of slit. Divide this measurement in half and add 1".

2. Mark this amount on bottom edge of material, as illustrated.

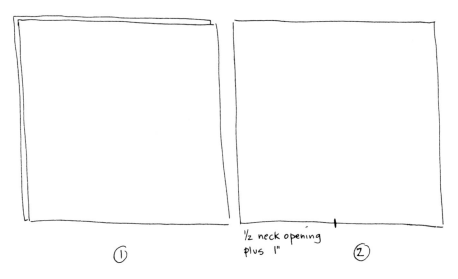

½ neck opening
plus 1"

① ②

3. Draw a diagonal line from top corner of material to first chalk mark, as illustrated. Pin over diagonal. Cut excess material past diagonal. Sew at top edge and over diagonal. Press seams. Turn ragged edges at seams and hem. Turn and hem other ragged edges.

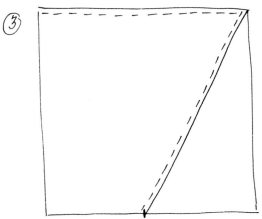

③

4. Align hood with kaftan, right side to right side, starting at one side of the kaftan's neck opening slit.

Pin hood to kaftan all the way around. Sew over pins. Remove pins.

If you wish to make your hood removable, sew about 5 snaps evenly around hood. Attach other end of snaps to neck opening aligning hood and neck.

For a Moroccan touch, add a tassle to the point of the hood

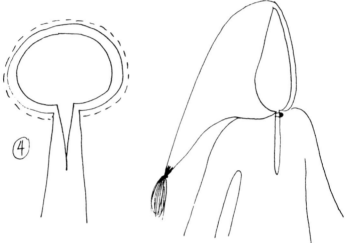

Materials for Kaftans:

Kaftan can be made of a variety of materials. For a house kaftan, choose something soft, maybe even sheer . . . or some material that can lap up water after a bath—terrycloth, for one.

For an outdoorsy kaftan—choose a medium-weight fabric, something that will stand up to the elements.

If your kaftan is to be used as an overcoat, choose a wool or some other warm, stiff material.

Ponchos

Easy Square Poncho:
1. Get a square of material 4' x 4'.
   Fold in quarters.
   Cut small curve at closed corner, as illustrated.

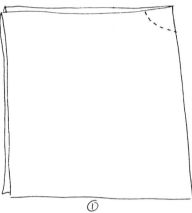

Neck Facing:
2. Cut a 1' square of scrap of material. Fold in quarters.

3. Lay facing over neck on poncho, matching the edges. Pin facing to poncho. Cut a curve in facing to match neck curve on poncho. Remove pins. Remove facing from poncho.

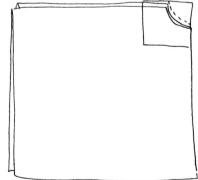

4. Cut the squared edge of facing from corner to corner, following contour of the curved end, as illustrated.

5. Open up the poncho. Open up the facing. Place facing to poncho, right to right side, matching holes. Pin facing to poncho ¼″ from holes. Sew over pins. Remove pins. Clip curves.

Facing is now on outside of poncho. Fold it inside. Trim edge if necessary. Turn ragged edges under and hem. Press.

You can wear this poncho with either the points or the squared edge in front.

Round Poncho:

Follow Easy Square Poncho Step 1.

1a. Cut a curve from corner to corner, as illustrated.

Follow Easy Square Step 2-5.

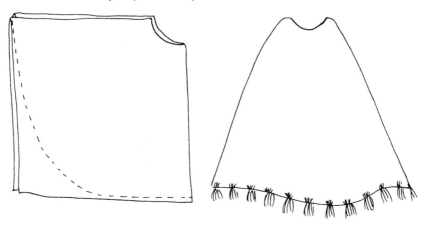

Long Poncho:

1. Get either a very large square of material (if you want poncho to cover your hands) or a rectangle of material 4' wide by whatever length you wish.

Fold in quarters.

Cut small curve at closed corner, as Easy Square Step 1.

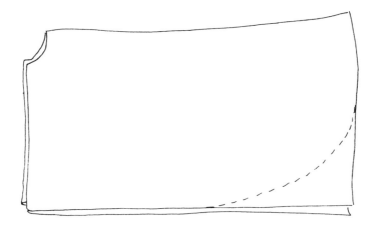

Follow Step 2-5 Easy Square Poncho.

When completed you can leave the poncho with its rectangular edges or round the edges off.

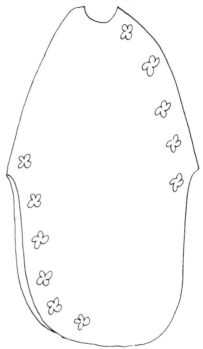

Cisco's Side Slit Poncho:

1. Cut a rectangle of material which is as wide as you are from shoulder to shoulder. Decide how long you want poncho (to hips, knees, ankles, floor). Double this length and add 6" for hemming.

Fold in quarters.

Cut small curve at closed corner, as illustrated Step 1 Easy Square Poncho.

Follow Step 2-5 Easy Square Poncho.

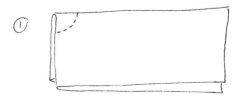

6. Fit poncho on.

Mark places where you want poncho to tie on both front and back. You may want a number of ties.

Sew ties to inside of poncho.

They can be made out of ribbon, leather or contrasting material.

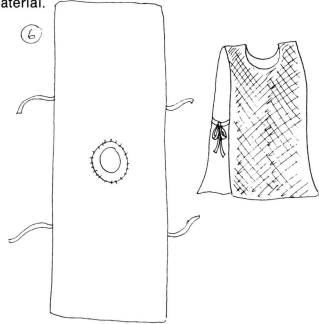

Poncho Necklines:

You can use any type of neck for your poncho. If you want it to have a hood, follow instructions for Top with Small Round Neck (with Slit in front) and then directions for Kaftan Hoods I or II.

Poncho Edgings:

Rickrack, tassles or embroidery are groovy on ponchos (see stitches).

Yarn tassles are nice on wool ponchos. If poncho is made of a light, clingy material, you can use ready-made silk tassles. For plaid ponchos, you can make the tassles out of multi-colored pieces of yarn.

Poncho Dresses

Mini-Monk's Dress:
1. Get a square of material 5' x 5'.

Fold in quarters.

Cut small curve at closed corner, as Step 1 Easy Square Poncho.

Follow Step 2-5 Easy Square Poncho.

6. Open poncho. Fold in half lengthwise, right side to right side.

Pin poncho along open edge, half way up, ½" from edge. Sew over pins. Remove pins. Press seams.

Turn poncho dress right side out. Turn ragged edges under and hem.

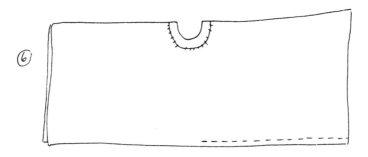

7. Step in to the dress carefully at top of seam. Put your

head through the neck hole. Throw remainder of poncho over your shoulders.

You might also want to add a matching or contrasting sash.

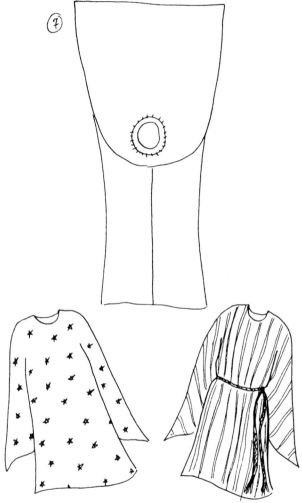

Angel Dress:

1. Get either a very large square of material (if you want dress to cover your hands) or a rectangle of material 4' wide by whatever length you wish.

Fold in quarters.

Cut small curve at closed corner, as Easy Square Poncho Step 1.

Follow steps 2-7 Short Poncho Dress.

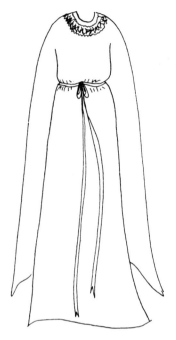

Materials for Ponchos:

Ponchos are so easy to make, they can be zipped up out of anything lying around. Use your judgment. For indoor occasions, make them out of light materials. For the outdoors, heavier materials.

Shawls, Scarves and Ties

Shawl

Get a piece of material as long as you want your shawl to be. If you buy this in a store, leave the width as is. This will save hemming the two longest edges. If you feel this width is too wide, fold in half when wearing.

Turn ragged edges under and hem.

That's it! Your shawl is completed. For variety, you can embroider on it or sew on tassles (see Stitches).

Scarf

It's best to make a scarf out of one piece of material, rather than using sewn-together scraps. The shape of your scarf depends on the size of your material.

Turn ragged edges under and hem.

1. If you have a large square scrap of material and nothing else to use it for, cut a diagonal strip out of center, as illustrated. This will form one long, flowing, Chelsea Antique Market-type scarf plus two small, triangular scarves.

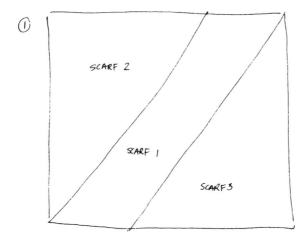

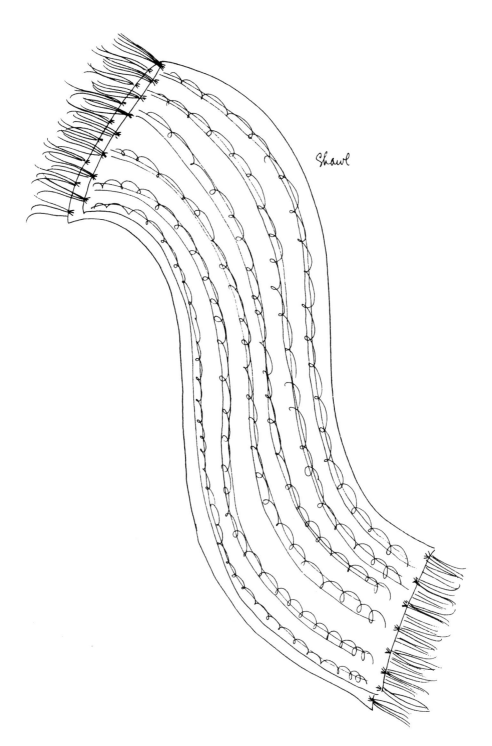

Shawl

2. Cut sides of each small, triangular piece to form an equilateral triangle. Turn ragged edges under and hem.

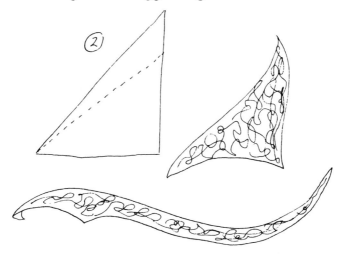

Note: Sharon bought a nickel piece of smooth, far-out whipped cream fabric on Orchard Street in New York City and got three scarves out of it in the above way.

Tie

1. Unless you are mathematically-inclined or have an excellent eye for accurate estimations, follow an old tie.

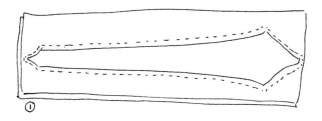

2. Use a piece of new material as long as the old tie, allowing extra material for seams and hems.

Get a piece of lining silk the same size as your material (lining silk is usually very cheap, about 50¢ a yard). Pin lining to material, right side to right side.

Remove stitching in back of old tie—carefully—and lay old tie flat for tracing.

Lay old tie over material. Pin and trace allowing a ½" seam allowance all around.

Remove pins. Remove old tie.

Cut material over chalk lines. Re-pin lining to material ½" from edge, leaving open the bottom, triangular edge. Sew over pins.

Turn tie right side out. You may need to push out the corners with a chopstick or pencil.

Turn edges under and hem. Press.

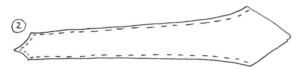

3. Fold the new tie exactly as the old tie was in the back. Hem back of new tie. (And hem back of old tie for re-use.)

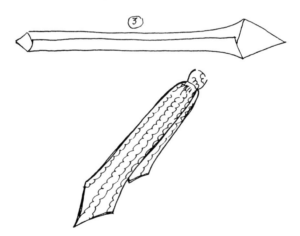

Materials for Shawls, Scarves and Ties:

Shawls and scarves should be made from flexible fabrics —softs and mediums, so that they adhere to the shape of your body. Ties, on the other hand, can flop about or stand out stiffly in front of you. Purple lace ties are always nice.

136

Little Goodies

Leather Pouches

Get together some scraps of soft leather and a medium-size leather needle. Use your imagination in designing the size and shape of your pouches. When sewing on pockets, use different leather and embroidery threads for contrasting colors.

Little Pouch:

1. Cut two identical rectangles of leather, whatever size you wish. Align these pieces, wrong side to wrong side.

2. Sew pieces together with embroidery thread, using either an overlap or blanket stitch on three sides (see Stitches).

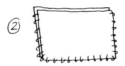

3. Get a zipper to fit the pouch opening. Align one side of zipper with inside of opening on either side.

Sew zipper to both sides using same stitch used in Step 2.

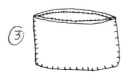

Flap Pouch:

    1. Cut a piece of leather as illustrated.

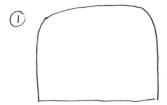

    2. Cut a rectangle of leather to match bottom half of first piece.

    3. Align these pieces wrong side to wrong side.

    Sew rectangle to first piece on 3 sides.

    Place "male" part of snap on inside of top flap. Sew. Sew "female" part of snap to outside of lower rectangle. Or, make a button and loop fastening (see Stitches).

    Stitch all around edges in contrasting thread for a decorative touch.

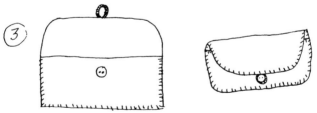

Roomy Pouch:

    1. Cut two identical squares or rectangles of leather.

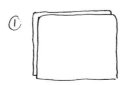

2. Measure three sides of your design and cut a strip of leather which is that length by 1 ½" wide.

Starting at the top of one side, align strip to leather piece, wrong side to wrong side.

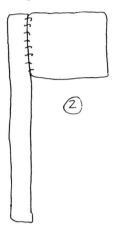

3. Sew strip around three sides, bending it at corners, as illustrated.

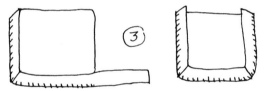

4. Sew other square or rectangle to strip as in Step 3.

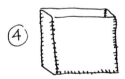

5. Sew in a zipper as in Step 3 of Little Pouch.

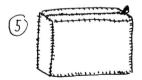

Roomy Pouch with Flap:

    1. Cut a piece of leather, as illustrated.

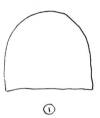

    2. Cut a rectangle of leather to match bottom half of first piece.

    3. Measure three sides of rectangle. Cut a strip of leather that length by 1 ½″ wide. Starting at the top of one side of rectangle, align strip to rectangle, wrong side to wrong side.

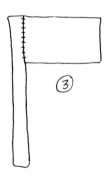

    4. Sew strip around three sides, bending strip at corners, as illustrated.

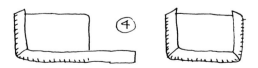

5. Sew flap piece to strip as in Step 4.

Sew on snaps as Step 3 in Flap Pouch, or use Button and Loop. Stitch all around edges in contrasting thread for a decorative touch.

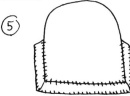

Note: If you have only small pieces of leather, sew a flap piece to a square or rectangle of leather at beginning of Step 1.

Pocket:

A pocket can be added on after Step 1 of any pouch, in the following way:

Cut a piece of leather which is smaller than the pouch side you are adding it to.

Lay wrong side of pocket to right side of pouch. Sew pocket to side on three sides, leaving top open.

Cloth Pouches

Little Cloth Pouch:

1. Cut two identical rectangles of material, whatever size you wish. Align these pieces right side to right side.

2. Pin together on three sides, ¼" from edge. Sew over pins. Remove pins.

3. Get a zipper to match size of pouch opening. Align one side of zipper with one side of opening, right side to right side. Sew zipper to material on both sides.

Turn pouch right-side up. To line this pouch: make another pouch, identical in size. Place lining inside pouch, wrong side to wrong side and stitch under zipper to hold in place.

Cloth Flap Pouch:

1. Cut a piece of material, as illustrated.

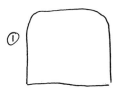

2. Cut a rectangle of material to match bottom half of first piece. Turn and hem top edge.

3. Align these pieces right side to right side, as illustrated.

Sew together on three sides. Turn pouch right-side out.

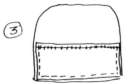

4. Turn and hem ragged edge of flap. Place "male" part of snap on inside of top flap. Sew. Sew "female" part of snap to outside of lower rectangle. Or, make a button and loop fastening (see Stitches).

Roomy Cloth Pouch:
1. Cut two identical squares or rectangles of material.

2. Measure three sides of squares or rectangles. Cut a strip of material that length by 1 ½" wide.

Starting at the top of one square or rectangle, align

strip to material, right side to right side. Pin strip all around the material, bending it at the corners.

Sew over pins, ¼" from edge, as illustrated.

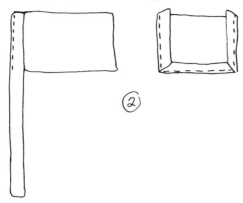

3. Sew other square or rectangle to strip as in Step 2. Sew in a zipper as in Step 2 of Little Cloth Pouch. Turn pouch right-side up.

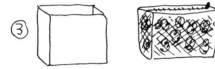

Pocket:

If you want to add a pocket, it should be added after Step 1, in the following way:

1. Cut a piece of material smaller than side of pouch you are adding it to. Hem ragged edge on top of pocket.

2. Lay wrong side of pocket to right side of material. Pin on three sides, tucking ragged edges under. Sew over and remove pins.

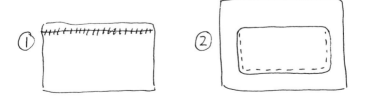

144

Cloth Bag

1. Cut a piece of material 1" x 25-30", depending what size bag you want.

Cut a strip of material 2" x 35-50" long, depending on whether you want a hand or shoulder strap.

2. Hem widthwise edges of first piece of material.

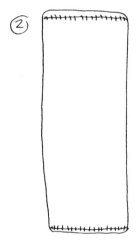

3. Fold first piece loosely, wrong side out, in thirds, to estimate what the size of the bag will be, as illustrated.

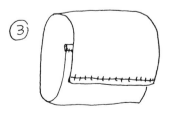

4. Pin strip piece to one side of bag, right side to right side. Sew, as illustrated, to each side of bag.

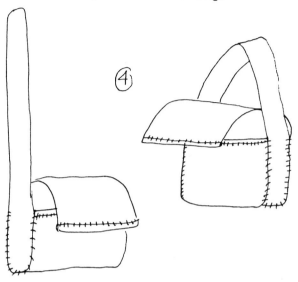

5. Turn bag right-side out.

Handle-Facing:

Cut a strip of material 2″ wide by length of bag handle from top edge of one side to top end of the other.

Place facing to handle, aligning right side to right side. Pin facing to handle down one side only, ½″ from edge. Sew over pins. Remove pins.

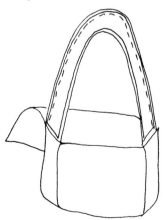

Your facing is now on the outside of your handle. Turn it under, aligning facing with open side of handle.

Turn in ragged edges of both facing and handle.

Hem open edge.

Sew snaps to flap, if you wish, following Step 4 Cloth Flap Pouch. You can add pockets to the inside of your bag by following instructions for Patch Pockets (page 57).

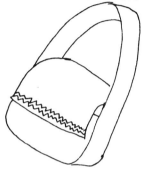

Tie Belt:

Measure waist or hips, wherever you want belt to lie.

Cut a strip of soft leather whatever width you choose by above length wide by length determined above plus some extra for fringing.

To fringe edges, cut lengthwise slits as close together as possible at both ends of belt.

Trim belt with embroidery (see Stitches) or sew on bits of leather.

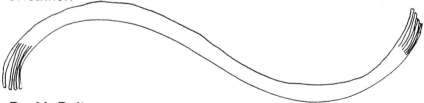

Buckle Belt:

Measure around your waist or hips, wherever you want belt to lie.

Cut a strip of leather the width you desire by above length plus 6" for overlap.

Attach one end of leather to buckle in the manner indicated by the type of buckle you get. You can either sew belt down over buckle or add snaps to make a detachable arrangement.

Trim, if you wish.

Note: If these belts are made out of material, remember to sew under ragged edges.

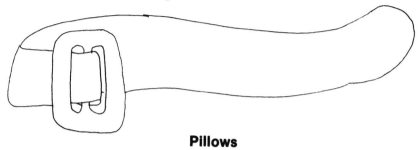

Pillows

Pillows are good to make from heavy material scraps—pieces of tapestry, felt, cut velvet, satin, heavy cotton, corduroy.

You can either recover an old pillow or make a new one, stuffing it with bits of foam, cork chips (cheaper and as nice as foam), kapok, or feathers. If your pillows are small, you can even stuff them with old stockings.

Pillow:

1. Take two identically-shaped pieces of muslin or other inexpensive material (any size or shape).

Place pieces right side to right side.

Pin together ½" from edge, leaving one side open for stuffing. (If making a circular pillow, leave an area open).

Sew over pins. Remove pins. Turn right-side out. Stuff to desired fullness or insert old pillow.

2. Sew up open side.

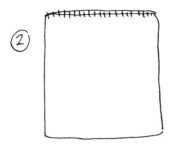

Pillow Cover:

1. Follow Step 1 as in Pillow above, using your groovy material. Place pillow into cover.

2. Neatly hem open edge of cover or close with snaps so cover can be removed for cleaning.

Sew tassles to 4 corners on square pillow for nice effect.

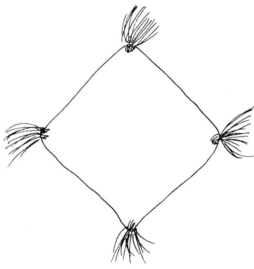

Pillow Case:

1. Follow Step 1 as in pillow.

2. Turn open edges under and hem ragged edges, or sew on snaps.

Trim pillows with rickrack, embroidery (see Stitches), lace or fringe at open edge.

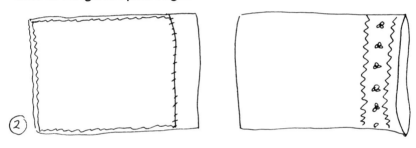

different pillows

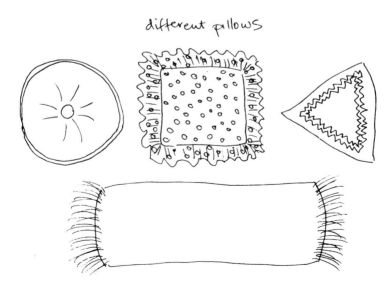

Clothes for Kids

It's really fun to make kids clothes because you get a whole, completed garment in a short time. And because they're so easy, you can embellish them richly with all kinds of things. First find out what kind of clothing the child you're sewing for digs. The worst thing is to make something to your own taste, rather than his. Kids have their own ideas about what they like to wear and, indeed, that's what they should wear—even if that means no bellbottoms, cute vests or suede fringe jackets, but rather Eton caps and blazers. Remember, it is they who are wearing it . . . not you folks.

Any of the garments from the book can be made to scale for kids, using the same methods as for adults. Just figure less time and less material.

sleeveless dress

hobbitop with speedboat neck

kiddy Kaftan

teeny weeny bikini

elastic top bell bottoms

poncho

short waistcoat with fringes

long waistcoat

flower top
with small
round neck

ten minute long skirt

sleeveless dress with ruffle bottom
with set in sleeves gathered at
shoulder and wrist

fly front pants
with pockets

Stuffed Childrens' Toys

Cut two identically-shaped pieces of material to resemble animals, vegetables, faces, flowers, people, anything.

Sew decorations to the right side of one piece, as suggested in illustrations. The decorations can be embroidered or sewn on.

Follow Steps for Pillow.

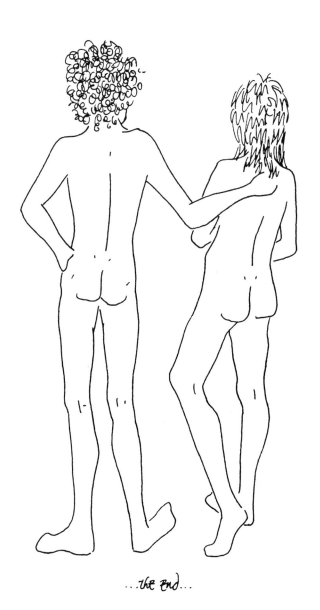

...the End...

154